BUSINESS ECONOMICS

John Charles Pool

The Durell Institute
a division of the
Harry F. Byrd, Jr. School of Business
at Shenandoah University

©1996 The Durell Institute
a division of the Harry F. Byrd, Jr. School of Business
at Shenandoah University
1460 University Drive, Winchester, VA 22601-5195

ISBN 1-882505-05-0

Printed in the United States of America

To my Mother,
Susan McKoin Thorp...
may she rest in peace.

Acknowledgments

Contrary to popular opinion, books like this one are the work of many more people than the author, who gets all the credit. This one, especially, involved the efforts of a large number of highly capable people, each of whom contributed in their own way.

First, I want to thank Elizabeth Racer, Director of the Durell Institute in the Harry F. Byrd School of Business at Shenandoah University, whose patience and vision has steered this series to new levels, project after project. Equal thanks goes to Dr. Daniel A. Pavsek, Dean of the Byrd School whose support and consultation was invaluable.

Kathryn Bryarly is the person who coordinated *everything*, with exceptional skill and patience. Martha S. Thorp copy-edited the manuscript with her usual skill and eye for detail. Then, there is the rest of the helpful staff of the Institute—especially Dianne Singer and Kathy Smith, who continue to perform logistical miracles. And finally, of course, we want to thank the late George Edward Durell whose benevolence and foresight made all this possible.

Professor Craig Hovey of Keuka College, the only person I have ever met who can make accounting seem simple and interesting, contributed Chapter 3 and co-authored the Student Study Guide along with Dr. Ross M. LaRoe of Denison University, my long-time friend and collaborator. Dr. LaRoe also did the complicated artwork displayed in the numerous charts and graphs.

Errors and omissions, which are probably numerous, are mine.

J.C.P.

Contents

Chapter 1
INTRODUCTION TO ECONOMICS

LEARNING OBJECTIVES

In this chapter we will learn about:
- ✓ Economics—what it is and what it is not.
- ✓ Scarcity and how it limits our choices.
- ✓ The various branches of economics and how they relate to each other.
- ✓ The four basic economic questions faced by every society.
- ✓ The four factors of production that work together to produce goods and services.
- ✓ What economics has to do with our personal and financial lives.
- ✓ The language and logic of economics.
- ✓ Some basic elements of the concept of costs.
- ✓ How scarce resources limit any society's production possibilities.

INTRODUCTION

We don't often think about it, but virtually everything we do all day, every day, is determined by economic forces. Even reading this book is costing you something, because you could be doing something else with your time. You have also made a decision to study instead of watching TV or doing something else that you enjoy. You are making an economic decision in the sense that studying represents a choice, or trade-off, between the benefits of studying economics and the satisfaction and enjoyment you could gain from another activity. You can't do everything you want, so you are forced to make choices. In fact, no one has the time, money, energy, knowledge, talent, and good luck to satisfy every possible desire. We all live in what economists call a context of scarcity. Scarcity exists everywhere because resources are limited. The entire planet, as we are increasingly aware, has limited resources—virtually everything is scarce. Can you name anything that isn't?

ECONOMICS: THE SCIENCE OF CHOICE

You have chosen to study economics, probably hoping that it will pay off in the long run with higher income and a more pleasant, meaningful, and productive life. It will, because when you get right down to it, every decision you make is in some sense an economic decision. Therefore, understanding economics will help you make more informed and rational choices as you go about the business of everyday life.

In this chapter we will first look at the scope of economics and its various branches. We will see how the complexities of our changing world make economics a useful, vital study. Then we will join some marooned islanders in their attempt to build a simple economy. We will come to understand the basic questions that they—and all societies—must deal with, including environmental issues. In particular, we will examine the various factors of production and a method for analyzing production possibilities among many different alternatives. And, not least, we will see how all economic issues are shaped by the reality of scarcity. But before we begin this excursion through the complex yet fascinating world of economics, we have to get some definitions straight. Let's start by defining economics and its major branches and examining their places in the world of ideas.

What Is Economics?

It is important to realize first of all that economics is one of the social sciences, the sciences of human behavior. Like political science, social psychology, sociology, and the other social sciences, economics tries to analyze human interactions objectively using scientific method, as any science does. This means (as shown in Figure 1-1) that economists make hypotheses, that is, formulate tentative theories, test them through experimentation against logic and reality, and then test them again and again. If, after enough testing, a hypothesis appears to fit with the facts, it then becomes part of accepted economic theory, ready to be used in managing businesses and developing economic policy.

 Key Concept: Scientific method is a procedure that uses experimentation to test hypotheses against reality.

But it is interesting and important to note that economics and the other social sciences differ from the so-called "hard sciences" in the sense that they must deal with human behavior, which is very difficult to predict. In the hard sciences—such as physics and chemistry—scientists work at least to some degree with a given set of known and predictable data they can assume to be

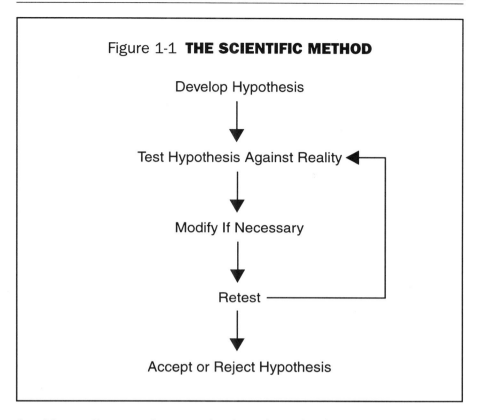

Figure 1-1 **THE SCIENTIFIC METHOD**

Develop Hypothesis

Test Hypothesis Against Reality

Modify If Necessary

Retest

Accept or Reject Hypothesis

fact. No one disagrees, for example, about the molecular composition of gold, but if you want to know what role gold should play as part of the money supply, you can find almost as many opinions as there are economists.

Economics, then, is first of all a social science that deals with human behavior, which is very difficult but not always impossible to predict. It is, therefore, a much less exact science than its mathematical trappings would suggest. Nevertheless, economics as a study can be specifically defined. In general, we can say that economics is the study of the production, distribution, and consumption of goods and services and environmental concerns, all in a context of scarcity.

Within its general framework, economics has two major branches—microeconomics and macroeconomics. Sometimes international economics is spoken of as a third branch, but it actually encompasses elements of both micro- and macroeconomics. The international sector was once relegated to a separate field of specialization, but now it tends to dominate all areas of economics—and all of our lives.

Microeconomics

As the name implies, **microeconomics** focuses on the smaller parts of the larger economy and on questions of efficient use of scarce resources. Microeconomics tries to show how each firm or consumer operates as efficiently and rationally as possible within the constraint that resources are scarce and budgets are limited. If resources such as land, labor, and technology were unlimited, they wouldn't cost anything, and there would be no need for a science that tries to determine how they can be utilized and distributed most efficiently. Microeconomics is easier to understand if you simply think about it as focusing on the behavior of small units in the economy such as a single business, a group of businesses that all produce the same product (an industry), or an individual or a group of consumers.

 Key Concept: Microeconomics is the study of the allocation of scarce resources among competing ends. It deals primarily with the operation of business firms and the behavior of consumers in a market setting.

Besides studying the behavior of firms and consumers, microeconomics is also useful in analyzing the issues of pollution, energy, labor, information and uncertainty, international trade, transportation, urban problems, public finance, government regulation, and the economics of the law. Although these topics may seem very different from each other, they all have to do with the allocation of scarce resources among competing ends.

Macroeconomics

By contrast, **macroeconomics** focuses on the economy as a whole—the aggregate of the decisions of millions of firms and individuals and government agencies. Macroeconomics deals with concepts like the gross domestic product (GDP), inflation, unemployment, economic forecasting, the consumer price index, overall savings, investment, and consumption. Macroeconomics also focuses on one major role of government in the economy: its role in spending and taxation (fiscal policy), and the role of the monetary system in facilitating the trade of goods and services (monetary policy).

 Key Concept: Macroeconomics is the study of the overall levels of employment, national output and income, and how they can be controlled.

Macroeconomics is what you read about on the front pages of your newspaper or see on the evening network news. When the headlines read

INFLATION RATE UP 2 PERCENT, or UNEMPLOYMENT HITS 7 PER-
CENT—as it did during the 1990–1991 recession—you are reading about
macroeconomic issues.

Macroeconomics tends to be strongly policy oriented. This has been especially true since World War II. The Employment Act of 1946 charged the
government with the task of keeping the economy running at full employment
without excessive rates of inflation. To do this the government and the monetary authorities have attempted to influence economic activities such as consumption, saving, and investment by manipulating such variables as government spending, tax rates, the supply of money available, and interest rates. As
it turns out, all this is considerably more difficult than it sounds on the sur-
face. But then, if it weren't, economics wouldn't be as challenging or interesting as it is.

International Economics

Another area which is part micro- and part macroeconomics is **international economics**. Until recently, however, it was only a small part of most
nations' total economic activity. In 1960, for example, the total value of U.S.
exports and imports was only 12 percent of the total U.S. economy. By 1995,
it was nearly 25 percent.

Key Concept: International economics is the study of the trading
of goods and services between nations and of the international
financial system that facilitates this trade.

The importance of international trade to the science of economics cannot be ignored if we are to understand our modern world. Fortunately, it is
easy to visualize because it affects our everyday lives. For example, the chances
are one in four that if you own a car, it was made in a foreign country. If you
own a stereo system, a VCR, or even a TV, the odds are almost 100 percent
that it was made in Japan or in one of the newly industrialized countries such
as South Korea or Taiwan that dominate the American electronic consumer-
goods market. The purchase of imported products is only one way international economics affects our everyday lives. Because of international trade,
we get better products at lower prices. But in the process, some argue that the
United States has lost millions of jobs to foreign competition in the past decade. That's an important issue, but one that we will not explore in great detail
here.[1]

---

[1]   International economics is the subject of our book and teaching kit entitled *EXPLORING
THE GLOBAL ECONOMY*, The Durell Institute, 1993.

Taken together, micro-, macro-, and international economics deal with the basic economic problems that every society must confront as it tries to conduct its economic affairs so as to maximize the standard of living for all of its citizens. But economics is much more than a way of thinking or of looking at events. Everything you do, as well as everything going on around you, has an economic aspect.

THE ECONOMIC PROBLEM: SHIPWRECK!

It's easier to understand and appreciate the complexity of economic systems if we look at a simple example first. Suppose we are on board a ship in the South Pacific. Alas, the ship is battered by a storm and it sinks. The crew and 40 surviving passengers (ourselves among them) make it safely to a deserted island and manage to salvage a few provisions from the ship. After taking stock of the disaster and the very likely prospect of being marooned for a long time, our group is forced to consider a number of obvious, yet difficult, questions.

First, we gather on the beach and begin to consider our basic needs: food, shelter, and clothing. During this meeting it is clear it will be difficult to provide even these essentials for survival, and that anything above and beyond the basics will have to wait. Everyone has a different idea of what is needed. But the reality is that the resources available on the island and the limited provisions recovered from the ship will dictate, at least in the short run, what needs and wants can be fulfilled. At this point our group realizes that the first question must be: WHAT SHOULD WE PRODUCE? Once this is addressed, the group will need to answer another difficult question: HOW SHOULD WE ORGANIZE PRODUCTION? Then, the group will confront one of the most difficult economic questions: HOW SHOULD WE DISTRIBUTE THE GOODS PRODUCED? Finally, the group will need to consider the issues of WHAT THEN?—how to deal with the problem of waste disposal as it uses the natural resources of the island. These are the basic economic questions and issues that every economic system must address. We might summarize them by asking: What? How? For whom? And, a relatively new concern: What then?

What to Produce

After extensive debate, the group agrees that the first several months the first priority will be to meet the basic needs of food, shelter, and clothing. A few people are assigned to do a quick inventory of the island resources to determine the options and possibilities for meeting basic needs. The island has abundant fresh water, fruit, nuts, herbs, fertile land, and, not surprisingly, good fishing. The tropical climate requires very little by way of shelter, yet everyone wants a separate dwelling and much more clothing than the climate demands. To a large extent it is clear our needs and wants are socially conditioned. Nevertheless, we finally reach agreement about what to produce, and the group moves on to the question of how should we organize production—who will do what?

How to Organize Production

The question of organizing production forces the group to consider the advantages and disadvantages of **specialization**. That is, should each member of the group take care of his or her own needs, or should the group assess individual skills and then divide the work according to these skills and the available tools and technology? In a sense, the group must consciously take the factors of production (land, labor, capital, and their technical and managerial skills) and organize them to produce the goods desired. Of course, there are many different ways to organize people to make clothing, shelters, and even to produce food.

 Key Concept: Specialization is the process of allocating specific tasks to different people to accomplish a given goal.

How to Distribute What is Produced

Let's assume that the group resolves the problem of organizing production by having those who know gardening focus on producing enough food so that everyone can eat, and letting those who know something about construction turn their efforts to building thatched-roof huts. But that creates another problem. What if one gardener is more efficient at producing food or is just lucky enough to find more fertile land and, as a result, is growing much more food than the others? Does the "farmer" get to keep it all or should it be shared equally with everyone else? Notions of justice indicate that the industrious hut builders should be fed. But we have another problem as well. A few lazy folks in the group are spending most of their time lying on the beach soaking up the sun, surviving by spearing a fish once in a while. How do we decide what to do with the surplus that our efficient farmers are producing?

One way to solve this problem of **distribution** would be to simply divide everything equally. But if we do that, our most efficient and hard-working—albeit lucky—gardeners may soon lose the incentive to work and start spending more time on the beach with the sun worshippers. Clearly, that plan would fail because soon there would be no surplus to share and we would all be hungry again.

Key Concept: Distribution is the process of allocating goods and services to various groups and individuals.

We've got to decide on another way to distribute the food surplus equitably. Offhand, it would seem fair to distribute the food to each person in an amount corresponding to how long each works no matter what the task. That way, those who contribute the most would also receive the most. That might work, but it would leave us with the problem of measuring the relationship between the amount of time worked and the amount of goods and services produced in that time. Thus we need a unit of measurement that stipulates how much work (at different rates of productive efficiency) is equal to how much food or whatever else is being produced, including the huts that are being built.

Suppose all this gets further complicated by our lazy beach bums, who discover that they can catch a few extra fish and trade them to the farmers for, say, some corn. How many fish, then, are worth one bushel of corn? At first, no one knows for sure, but a bit of bargaining between two traders soon establishes a barter "price" that represents some ratio between how long it takes to catch one fish and how long it takes to grow a bushel of corn. That seems reasonable because both the fisher and the farmer get in trade an amount consistent with the amount of labor each performed to produce the product. But one day someone finds a fishing net washed up on the beach. This lucky fisher can now catch 10 times as many fish as when he used a spear like everyone else. Things are really getting complicated.

Now suppose we have decided that everyone is entitled to keep—that is—to own, the fruits of his or her labor. By doing this, we have established a system of **private property**, which allows people to do whatever they wish with the product of their labor, including selling it, or destroying it, or accumulating it for future use. So what will our lucky net owner do?

Key Concept: Private property is a system in which individuals have the right to keep, use, or sell the goods they produce or legally acquire.

With more fish than one person can possibly use, the net owner is soon trading fish to all the farmers on the island and thus accumulating all the surplus corn. Now, anyone who wanted either fish or corn must come to this one person and offer something to trade for it. If they have nothing to trade, they can trade their labor and start working for the net owner—casting the net or bringing in and dressing the fish. The net owner is becoming the richest person on the island. Things are growing even more complicated. But nobody ever said capitalism was simple.

Resource Use and Disposal

With the fundamental questions of production, organization, and distribution at least temporarily resolved, the group now must consider the ways in which even its simple economic system affects the natural environment. After using the natural resources of the island—what then? How will different production methods and technologies, not to mention the consumption and disposal of goods, affect our physical environment? For example, should we let fish heads pile up for the gulls to eat, or should we throw them over a cliff where the currents will carry them to a neighboring island? And if we choose the latter, will the neighbors—if there are any—object? Fortunately, several members of the group have studied environmental science. These folks are designated by the group to evaluate the environmental consequences of the production system and to study the available resources on the island in terms of current and projected uses.

Inter-island Trade

After six months, several large canoes appear on the horizon. The group gathers on the beach in anticipation of rescue, hoping that the visitors will be friendly, for they have made no plans for defense.

The first canoe beaches and a friendly fellow disembarks and says, smiling, "Hi, folks! What you got to trade?"

"Well, I've got some extra corn," our fishnet owner says. "What have you got?"

"Nothing today but fishnets," the friendly fellow replies. "I've got about forty."

The moral of the story: international trade sure does make things complicated.

THE FACTORS OF PRODUCTION

It should be clear from this little story that every society faces complicated problems when it comes to deciding the most basic economic questions of all: what, how, for whom, and what then, all of which must be taken in the context of scarcity. Further, whenever goods and services are produced, four basic factors are involved: **land, labor, capital, and the entrepreneurial skill** to utilize them to produce needed goods and services. The latter is commonly called entrepreneurship. We need to look at these factors of production in some detail if we are to understand how business works.

Key Concept: The factors of production are land, labor, physical and financial capital, and the entrepreneurial skill to get them organized to produce goods and services.

Land

It's easy to understand that whenever anything is to be produced, a certain amount of space is needed in which to make it or in the case of food, to grow it. Note, however, that the word land should not be taken literally. It refers to much more than the land we walk on. In economics land means climate, oceans, grazing land, rivers, harbors, and much more. Clearly, land is essential for production, whether we're talking about simple space or the natural resources that land provides. In any case, it is a very limited resource. There's only so much land in the world, and good land with fertile soil, mineral resources, or a good location for trade is even more limited. No wonder that, historically, great fortunes have been based on land ownership and wars have been fought over it.

Labor

People must work if anything is to be produced. Imagine a society with leadership, equipment, and plenty of land, but where no one is willing to work. Traditionally, however, labor has been the most plentiful of the factors of production. The pyramids of Egypt were built with simple technology but plentiful labor. In modern times, however, technology often reduces the amount of labor needed for a job. One effect of replacing people with machines has been an increase in the productivity of each worker. That increased productivity—higher output per hour of labor—has generally led to a higher standard of living.

Labor is not just a willingness to work but also the ability to work—that is, skill level. People can "rent out" skills to an employer or use them for their own projects. Either way, labor has value and a market price based on demand for various skills, just as land has a value based on the demand for its use.

Capital

Capital, which is also needed for production, is a less obvious concept. Capital consists of the buildings, machinery, and tools that are needed, whether it be a simple hoe or screwdriver or a complex computerized robot on an automobile assembly line. But capital also refers to the money that must be accumulated, or borrowed, to pay the other factors of production until the product is sold. The distinction between physical capital—capital goods—and financial capital—money and credit—is an important one, worth remembering as we examine these concepts in more detail later.

Entrepreneurship

The fourth factor of production, entrepreneurship and managerial skill, is needed any time the production of anything takes place. You don't just build an automobile in your garage; a lot of special knowledge is involved, as well as land, labor, and real and financial capital. This function is called **entrepreneurship**. Entrepreneurship may be technical knowledge or it may be managerial skill coupled with the willingness to take risks. But whatever it's called, it is still knowing how to organize the factors of production to accomplish a given goal, which varies from society to society depending mostly on the accumulated level of technology.

 Key Concept: Entrepreneurship is the ability to combine land, labor, and capital with technological know-how to produce goods and services with the objective of profit and the risk of loss.

The person who starts up a new business is called an entrepreneur (from a French word meaning "to undertake"). Besides (often) taking a managerial role, entrepreneurs are compensated for their vision, skill, hard work, knowledge, leadership, and willingness to take risks by receiving the profits or absorbing any losses from the enterprise. Throughout the rest of this text this fourth factor of production is simply called entrepreneurship.

Realizing that there are many factors involved in the production process helps us understand that every community and every nation must deal with the fact that it has a limited amount of resources and a limited level of technology to apply to producing goods and services. Choices must be made. If a country decides to produce tanks, then it can manufacture fewer automobiles, and so on. In a complex industrialized society such as the United States, individuals, businesses, and society as a whole must make thousands of these decisions every day. One of the tasks of economists is to analyze how those decisions can be made rationally toward the goal of maximizing production and the general welfare, given that resources are scarce even in a rich country like ours. This task is quite complex, and different countries approach it in different ways.

CAPITALISM

As we could see from our simple example of the marooned islanders, the economic problem of organizing production is not, in fact, so simple. The solution not only determines how efficient the society can be in allocating its scarce resources, but it also establishes the rules and framework for determining the distribution of goods and services.

In recent decades, especially since the reorganization of the Soviet Union and the fall of the Berlin Wall, capitalism has become the dominant economic model throughout the world, with only a few exceptions.

The Market Economy

Capitalism is an economic system based fundamentally on private ownership of the means of production. It is a system that develops private markets for land, labor, services, capital, and entrepreneurship and is driven by competition between producers. Economic decisions are made by free markets. That is, under a capitalist system of economic organization, decisions are in one sense simplified—and in another complicated—by the fact that decisions about what to produce are, for the most part, made by the free, unfettered operation of the market system. In a free market, anything can be produced. Whether it will continue to be produced depends on how well it stands the test of the market. If consumers want it and are willing to give up thousands of other consumption opportunities to buy it, then it will be produced. If it doesn't sell, it won't be produced for very long.

Key Concept: Capitalism is an economic system based on private ownership of the factors of production and on free markets that determine what should be produced.

Thus, in a capitalist system the consumer ultimately makes the decision about what will be produced, which is why we sometimes say "the consumer rules" or "the customer is always right." Capitalism is a system where **consumer sovereignty** prevails. That the consumer is king or queen is one of the basic tenets of a capitalist economy. Capitalism gives us needed products, like hospitals and automobiles, and some that are not so needed, like gambling casinos and illegal drugs. Consumer sovereignty gives us what we want because if we didn't want it badly enough to buy it, the product wouldn't be produced.

Key Concept: Consumer sovereignty is the idea that decisions about what to produce are dictated by consumers' desires.

For the individual, the distribution of income under capitalism is theoretically determined by the value of a person's labor, capital, land, or entrepreneurship. Because these factors of production vary in value, one person's standard of living may be quite different from someone else's. In a capitalist economic system the role of government is theoretically limited to a few basic functions required for an efficient and productive market system, such as national defense and highways.

THINKING STRAIGHT ABOUT ECONOMICS

Having examined some of the basic issues in economics and defined some important terms and concepts we need to pause and consider that economics is a science based on certain principles and methods. That means, in effect, that economics has its own language and logic—just like all sciences. Before we proceed, we need to examine some basic concepts that help us "think straight" when it comes to business and economics.

Correlation and Causation

It is easy to think that because two different events or processes seem related, one must cause the other. Watch out for this trap. It has been our observation over the years that most of the best economists eat a lot of pretzels. Does that mean eating pretzels somehow makes a person a good economist? Hardly. To think so is to confuse correlation with causation. It may be possible to scientifically analyze why a person is a good economist, but any careful analysis would have to reject pretzel consumption as cause.

Another interesting example is the 55 miles per hour speed limit. When the speed limit was reduced in the 1970s it was assumed that there would be fewer highway accidents and fatalities, and there were. But was the cause due to the lower speed limit, or to other factors? The lower speed limit meant that fewer people used auto transportation because it took longer than before to get from one place to another. With fewer people traveling the highways there were fewer accidents. Which was the cause and which was the correlation? The answer is not clear. All we know is that there is correlation; the cause may or may not have been the lower speed limit.

During the late 1800s English economist William Stanley Jevons theorized that business cycles were related to the intensity of sun spots—the fire storms on the sun. He was roundly criticized by his fellow economists for confusing correlation with causality. But meteorologists later discovered that sun spots do affect the weather on earth, and since the weather affects agricultural production, which affects the economy, Jevon's theories (although eventually discarded) had to be reconsidered.

There are many similar examples. It has been determined that the general health of the economy is closely correlated to the length of women's hemlines. The economy generally is booming when skirts are short but falters when they are long. Do mini-maxi fashions affect the economy? Of course not. But there is a strong correlation nonetheless.

Even more frivolous is the popular notion that the stock market goes up whenever a team from the old National Football League wins the Super Bowl game. And the market goes down when an American League team wins. The correlation is extremely close, but we'll leave it to you to decide if there is a causal relationship between football games and the stock market. In any case, it is easy to confuse correlation with causality. This is a pitfall to be avoided at all costs if we are to construct good theories that have value in the real world.

Fallacies of Composition

An even more common error that sometimes creeps into theoretical constructions and discussions is the assumption that what works for one will work for all. There are many examples. If you are in the stands at a hockey game and want a better view of the action, you should stand up. But what happens if everyone stands up? Obviously, what works for one doesn't work for all, which is why standing up at a sports event is not a very good strategy. If you want to get a good parking space at work, one way to do it is to get there early. But that won't help if everyone else has the same idea. If there is a fire alarm, the quickest way to get out of your classroom is to jump up and run out the door. Yet, if everyone did that, you would probably be crushed by other frantic students. Would you like to get away from the congestion of the big city? Then move to the suburbs; but by now you already know what would happen if everybody has the same theory. To think that what works for one will work for all is a **fallacy of composition**—meaning the composition of the issue is not correct.

 Key Concept: A fallacy of composition is the logical error of assuming that what may work for one will work for all.

To take another example, it is almost universally recognized that a household must save its money and live within its means. Otherwise, it will go into debt and may eventually go into bankruptcy. By the same reasoning almost as many people believe that a government must live by the same rules. But most economists agree that that's not the case. Households generally have fixed incomes and, since its members don't plan to work forever, must save for retirement. But governments—within some limits—don't face the same constraints. Governments can increase their income by increasing taxes, and governments don't have to save for retirement because they (usually) exist in perpetuity. So to think that governments and households must live by the same rules is a (very common) fallacy of composition.

Ceteris Paribus

One final potential pitfall that most economists and, indeed, all scientists agree must be avoided in order to develop coherent, usable theories is the notion that experimentation must be conducted under the rule of *ceteris paribus*. This Latin term, translated literally, means "everything else being equal." To test a theory for validity, reliability, and predictability, we must change the variables one at a time. Suppose you catch a cold and want to take something to feel better. You take some aspirin, a decongestant, a large dose of Vitamin C, some chicken soup, and a lot of other liquids, and you feel better. Your theory that these remedies would help is apparently correct. But, in applying your remedies you don't know which one helped, and the next time you catch a cold you'll need to apply all of them all over again. The only way you could develop a valid cure-for-colds theory that would have any value to you or anyone else would be to try your remedies one at a time, keeping everything else constant. It would take longer but, eventually, you would know exactly what it was that made you feel better.

 Key Concept: *Ceteris paribus* means that in experimental situations only one variable at a time can be changed while all others are held constant.

In any scientific experiment, everything else must be held constant while only one variable is changed. In economics, where hundreds of constantly changing variables may be involved, then scientific experimentation may not be so simple, but it is usually possible. Economic theories are tested all the time in a variety of different settings. Microeconomic theories of consumer behavior have been tested on everything from rats to humans. Macroeconomic theories are harder to test because we can't just stop the economy and then start it again after we have changed one variable, but such tests are conducted all the time. One of the more interesting recent examples was the Reagan administration's experiment with tax reduction—to which we shall return later. Ronald Reagan was convinced that high taxes discouraged people (and businesses) from working hard. Therefore, he and his economic advisors convinced Congress that a tax cut would so stimulate economic activity that the government would end up collecting more tax revenues even if taxes were lowered. To many people this seemed contrary to common sense, but the experiment was carried out anyway.

To sum up, most economists agree that for economic theory to have much legitimacy, it must distinguish between causation and correlation; it must avoid fallacies of composition; and it must be tested under *ceteris paribus* conditions. But even then it doesn't always follow that IF-THEN will always lead to a THEREFORE.

OPPORTUNITY COSTS

One thing that all economists agree on is that the concept of **opportunity cost** permeates all economic theories and issues. Understanding this idea, which is at once both simple and complex, is crucial to understanding economics. A bit of extra time now making sure you have it mastered will pay big dividends as you work your way through the rest of this book.

 Key Concept: Opportunity cost is the cost of the next best foregone alternative.

Since you are reading this, you have already made an economic decision. You have decided to use your time to read economics instead of reading something else, watching TV, or even, perhaps, working. Suppose, for example, that you could be earning some money now working somewhere. Then the cost of reading this chapter is equal to the money you could have earned during the time it took you to read it. You passed up an opportunity to make some money to learn something about economics instead. When you get right down to it everything we do involves a decision to pass up the opportunity to do something else. So the cost of doing anything is equal to what we could have gotten out of doing something else, either in monetary terms or just in terms of the satisfaction you lost by not doing it. The value of the next best foregone opportunity is called the "opportunity cost." The concept has important uses. In fact, it helps us clarify decision making both in business and in our personal lives.

Accountants versus Economists

Suppose you are pondering whether to go to college. What will it cost? Ask an accountant and you will hear that the cost will be the sum of the cost of tuition, fees, books, and transportation. Those, obviously, are your direct costs. But ask an economist and you will be told that the cost of going to college will be somewhat higher than the accountant said it would be. It will equal everything the accountant added up for you plus the amount you could earn if you worked full time instead of going to college. Anyone who works for a year, even at a minimum wage of $4.25 an hour, will earn $8,840. That's not a small consideration.

In other words, if you decide to go to college and pass up the opportunity to work, you are investing not only in the explicit costs of tuition and so on, but you are also paying the implicit costs of forgoing the opportunity to work. Added together these costs make going to college a lot more expensive than one commonly thinks. Of course, this is a short-run versus long-run proposition. If you go to college, you are probably betting that the short-run investment will pay off in higher income in the future. All the data show that it will, but interestingly not by as much as is commonly thought when opportunity costs are taken into account.

In a business context an understanding of opportunity costs is crucial to all decisions. Suppose you own and operate a small grocery store. At the end of the year your accountant adds up your total sales and they equal $100,000, while your direct expenses are $80,000. Obviously you have made a profit of $20,000. Not too bad, considering that you also probably get some satisfaction out of being your own boss. However, perhaps you should now consult your neighborhood economist. If you do, you will be dismayed to learn that although it may look on paper as if you made a profit, in actual fact, you probably didn't. Why? Because you forgot to take into account your opportunity costs—the highest income you could have earned by working elsewhere. If, in this example, you are a skilled grocery manager, chances are you could have earned more than $20,000 working for some large grocery chain. If you could have earned, say, $30,000 doing that, you have lost $10,000 in opportunity costs by being in business for yourself.

To put it another way, if you decide to stay in business, the income you lost is equal to the psychological satisfaction you get out of being self-employed. In pure economic terms, it's not a very rational decision, and it never will be unless you can increase your profits to the point that they equal your next best opportunity, that is, your opportunity costs. So the next time you have to make a rational decision about what to do with your time, you might be well advised to call on a friendly economist. Or you could just ask yourself, "Is this course of action going to cover my opportunity costs?"

Opportunity Costs and Social Choices

Opportunity costs also show up in other ways. They underlie almost all the debates in Congress over how to allocate the limited federal budget. Do we want to spend $1 billion on building a new dam and water-reclamation project? Then we have to give up building two Stealth bombers. Do we want a catastrophic health-care insurance program? Then we have to give up repairing and modernizing the interstate highway system, and so on. Given that any society has limited resources, that is, faces scarcity, then any social choice involves trade-offs. The real cost of doing anything is the cost of the next best opportunity that must be foregone. That's why economists say that real costs are foregone costs.

Production Possibility Frontiers

The concept of opportunity costs is perhaps best illustrated by the use of an important concept called a production possibility frontier. Any society faces a menu of choices from which it must choose as it allocates scarce resources to produce needed goods and services. The opportunity cost of producing more of one is producing less of another.

To take a simple example, suppose that the group of marooned islanders we met earlier faced the choice of spending all their time fishing or picking coconuts. If they devoted all their resources to fishing they could catch 200 fish a week, as shown in Figure 1-2, point A, where there were no coconuts being harvested. Then suppose that the group decided to assign some of their members to picking coconuts instead of fishing. If they pick 25 coconuts the number of fish being caught falls to 180, as shown at point B. So the real cost

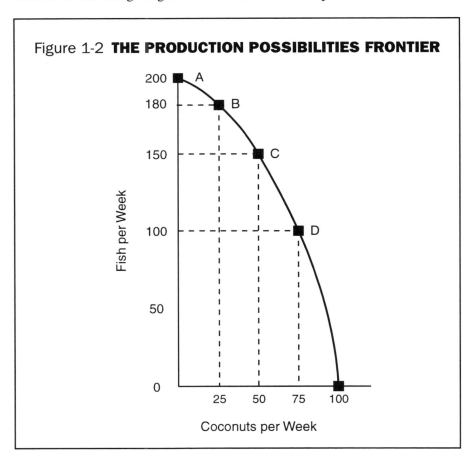

Figure 1-2 **THE PRODUCTION POSSIBILITIES FRONTIER**

of that choice is the opportunity cost of not fishing (20 fish) balanced by the gain of picking coconuts (25 coconuts).

Of course, several other options are available as shown at point C and D (in Figure 1-2). Allocating resources at point C yields 150 fish and 50 coconuts, whereas point D yields 100 fish and 75 coconuts. Every change in the mix of resources involves the cost of other opportunities forgone. This is the choice all societies face as they allocate resources among thousands of competing uses and opportunities. But, whatever the case, this society cannot produce at point F, which is beyond its production possibilities frontier. Why? Because the frontier defines its production limits given its available resources and technical know-how.

WHAT DOES THIS HAVE TO DO WITH ME?

With this brief overview, we can see how understanding economics may help us in our careers and in our role as consumers. It may even help us earn more money, but there is a lot more to economics—and to life—than that.

To be intelligent and responsible citizens, we must understand the economics behind the political issues that dominate every election—national, state, or local. Should taxes in general be reduced? If so, why? Or why not? What rate of interest will keep the economy growing? Should the minimum wage be raised? The Japanese have purchased CBS Records, Columbia Pictures, and Rockefeller Center. Is this good for us or does it represent a gradual selling out of the country's assets to foreign interests? These questions and many more are issues that cross the boundaries between politics and economics. What do they have to do with us? Everything. They are the issues of our lives, our welfare, and our future.

SUMMARY

✓ Why is economics important to our everyday lives? Because virtually everything we do involves economic decisions.

✓ Economics is a social science that attempts to explain, interpret, and predict human behavior using scientific method.

✓ One major branch of economics—microeconomics—deals with the efficient allocation of scarce resources among competing ends. It focuses on consumers, households, and business firms, all of whom have to make decisions in a market setting while confronted with the reality of scarcity.

✓ The other major branch of economics—macroeconomics—deals with overall levels of economic activity and attempts to explain how variables such as consumption, investment, and government spending can be influenced toward the goal of full employment without excessive rates of inflation.

✓ International economics, which encompasses both micro and macro issues and theories, focuses on the increasingly important exchange of goods and services across national borders and on the financial system that facilitates this trade.

✓ In its simplest terms, economics is mostly concerned with four basic questions all societies face: what to produce, how to produce it, who to distribute it to, and how to protect the natural resources we depend on. This means economics must deal with the efficient utilization of the factors of production: land, labor, capital, and entrepreneurship, which includes managerial skills, technological knowledge, and the willingness to take risks.

✓ Under a capitalist system decisions about production and distribution are usually made by the unobstructed free-market system, which allocates resources to where they are most needed or wanted.

✓ One key to thinking straight about economics is to remember that just because two events seem to be related, correlation is not the same as causation.

✓ To be reliable, economic theories must be tested under conditions of *ceteris paribus*, where everything is assumed to be equal and variables are changed one at a time.

✓ Opportunity costs permeate our lives at every turn. Anything we do has costs because we gave up something else to do it. This trade-off is the key to all business decisions.

✓ Production possibility frontiers define the outer limits of what any society can produce with a given level of resources.

✓ To come full circle, what all this has to do with us is that economics can help us understand how the world works; how to be more efficient, productive, and successful in our private lives and careers; to be more intelligent and responsible citizens and voters; and to be better consumers and business people.

NEW VOCABULARY

scarcity	private property
scientific method	factors of production
economics	capitalism
microeconomics	consumer sovereignty
macroeconomics	fallacy of composition
international economics	*ceteris paribus*
specialization	opportunity costs
distribution	production possibility frontiers

QUESTIONS FOR REVIEW

1. What is the relationship between making economic choices and the concept of scarcity?

2. What is the basic definition of economics?

3. What is the scientific method? How would you apply the scientific method to an economic problem? Give an example.

4. Define each of the following: (a) microeconomics, (b) macroeconomics, (c) international economics. How are they related to each other?

5. What are the four basic economic questions faced by every society?

6. What are the basic factors of production? How do they work together to produce goods and services? Think of an example.

7. History shows that there is a high correlation between economic recessions and a new president being elected. Do new presidents cause recessions?

8. What could cause a production possibility frontier to shift outward?

9. Suppose you decide to get a haircut and it takes about an hour. How much did the haircut cost you?

10. Why is the study of economics important to our personal lives?

Chapter 2
BUSINESS ORGANIZATION

LEARNING OBJECTIVES

In this chapter we take a brief look at the capitalist system, explore how it works, and why.

- ✓ First we look at capitalism and entrepreneurship and how it relates to starting and running a business.
- ✓ Then we look at the role of entrepreneurs, the capitalists who risk their time and money to start new companies in the hope of making profits.
- ✓ After that we examine how and why businesses are organized into sole proprietorships, partnerships, or corporations.
- ✓ Then we examine the details of starting a new company, issuing stock, and selling it to the public.
- ✓ Finally, we look at some of the nitty-gritty of the financial aspects of running a company with a focus on understanding annual reports and financial statements.

INTRODUCTION

How Capitalism Works

As we saw in the first chapter, capitalism is an economic system in which everything needed to produce good or services is owned by private individuals, as opposed to the only other alternative, being owned by the government. And we saw that in order to produce any product—any good or service—four things are required. One is land, by which is meant some space and/or some natural resources. Another is labor, people willing to spend their time working on the production of the product. Another is capital, the plant and equipment (usually tools and machinery) needed. And, finally, we need the know-how to do it—the technical knowledge and skills necessary to combine the other factors together efficiently to produce the product. But more than mixing these resources goes on in our capitalist system. Money is involved, and so is risk.

ENTREPRENEURSHIP

Money is required to buy and control the factors of production, and those who put up the money run the risk of losing it. Those who are willing to invest their money in a business are called entrepreneurs. They may be people who own businesses and employ others to manage it, or they may also run the business. Either way they bear the risk of losing their investment if the business doesn't succeed. Of course, they share in the profits if it does well.

You don't have to be an entrepreneur to participate in the capitalist system. Indeed, most of us are involved in capitalism in other ways. For example, we can buy land and rent it to entrepreneurs. Or, we can sell our labor and work for a wage or salary, which is the most common way most of us participate. Or, we can lend money to a company or individuals and receive interest payments. Or, we can buy stock and become a part owner of a company, in which case we share the profits—and the losses—with the entrepreneur who started it. The latter is our primary concern here.

FORMS OF BUSINESS ORGANIZATION

In the United States, businesses are normally organized according to the pattern of ownership they adopt. The simplest and most common form of ownership is the sole proprietorship, followed by partnerships, and by corporations—the form of organization usually adopted for large businesses.

Sole Proprietorships

As the name implies, **sole proprietorships** are normally businesses owned by one individual who bears sole responsibility for its operation. Most small businesses such as small retail stores, barbershops and beauty salons, and farms are organized this way. Indeed, there were some 13 million sole proprietorships in the United States in 1996, or about eighty percent of the total business population.

 Key Concept: Sole proprietorships are businesses owned by one individual who bears total responsibility for its operation.

Sole proprietorships have many advantages, but some disadvantages. The advantage is that the business is easy to set up, requiring in most cases only a local low-cost "Doing Business As" (DBA) county license. Sole proprietorships are simple but attractive in the sense that one person is "the boss," able to run the business how and when he or she wishes. This advantage—that of "being your own boss," is one reason many people prefer to run sole proprietorships even when they could make more money working for someone else. In this sense, the loss of income attributed to being your own boss is sometimes called "psychic income" because of the satisfaction it brings the owner. If the business is profitable, being able to keep all the profit instead of having to share it with someone else is, of course, another advantage.

The disadvantage of being a sole proprietor is that while you may be able to keep the profits, you also bear all the risk. In fact, legally, the owner faces unlimited liability for business debts and other responsibilities such as job-related injuries. That means if the business fails, the owner's personal property—house, car, and other assets—can be seized by creditors. This is the primary reason many business are organized in more complex forms.

Partnerships

The next simplest way to organize a business is the **partnership**. Many law firms, engineering and architectural firms, and other business firms are organized as partnerships. In 1996 there were about one million businesses organized this way: about ten percent of all businesses in the nation.

 Key Concept: Partnerships are businesses owned by two or more persons who share responsibility for it.

In many ways, the partnership is similar to the sole proprietorship in the sense that it is easy to set up and administer. But the advantage in partnerships that two or more people bring different skills and specializations to the firm. Often one partner will have sales and marketing skills, while the other has managerial or accounting skills.

The disadvantage is that all of the partners in the firm share equally in the risks and liabilities of the firm. Therefore, except for professional occupations, partnerships are not a common form of business organization for large companies.

Corporations

In terms of size and total sales, **corporations** are the dominant form of business organization in the United States. There are about 2 million corporations in the country, but they account for nearly ninety percent of the total sales of goods and services in the economy. Indeed, the top 500 largest corporations account for nearly 50 percent of the Gross Domestic Product.

Key Concept: Corporations are businesses that have the same legal responsibility as others but are owned by a group of stockholders who appoint managers to be responsible for the operation of the business.

The primary reason for organizing a large company as a corporation is that, while it functions as a person in the eyes of the law, no one individual is legally responsible for its actions. Corporations are owned instead by many different people and organizations—its stockholders—who share the financial risk if the price of its shares falls, but they are not legally responsible for the corporation's actions. Instead, the corporation is.

The biggest advantage of corporate organization is that the owners face limited liability. If the corporation goes bankrupt, its owners (stockholders) only lose what they have invested and cannot be sued by the company's creditors. Another advantage is that corporations can raise money to invest in expanding the business by issuing stock or issuing bonds.

One disadvantage is that setting up a corporation is relatively complicated compared to sole proprietorships and partnerships and, as we shall soon see, the accounting and reporting obligations are relatively detailed and often complex, and usually require the help of an accountant. Another is that as opposed to sole proprietorships and partnerships, ownership and management are generally separated. As we shall see below, the owners (stockholders) elect a Board of Directors that, in turn, appoints management to run the company. Managers may or may not also be stockholders, although most are. Finally, there is the question of taxes. Sole proprietors and partnerships pay taxes only on profits. Corporations must pay corporate tax on their profits just as an individual does, but the stockholders must also pay individual taxes on whatever amount they receive as dividends from those profits. Many economists and others have criticized this as "double taxation" and believe the tax laws should be changed accordingly.

CORPORATE STOCKS

When you buy stock in a corporation you become a part owner of it. That means you own a small (probably very small) part of anything those companies own, be it a building, some machinery, or a car or truck. It also means you own a share of any money it may have in the bank. And it means you have a right to share in any dividends that company paid out of its profits, and a right to voice your opinions about how the company is managed. However, you also share the risk that the company may lose money, which means the value of its stock may fall or, at worst, the company can go bankrupt, causing you to lose your investment.

Issuing New Stock

Why would a company want to sell part of itself to outside investors? Why would it let you have a say in how the company is run? Because, at some point it needed to raise money, either to get the company started or to expand its operations in an attempt to increase its profits.

Before we examine that process, we need to repeat that the word "capital" has two meanings. **Capital** refers to the plant and equipment (such as buildings and machinery) needed in the production process. But, the word capital also describes the money required to buy and control the factors of production. Thus, there is a distinct and important difference between these two definitions: real, or physical capital is one thing; financial capital is another.

 Key Concept: Capital has two meanings: real capital is plant and equipment; financial capital is the money needed to control the factors of production.

Usually corporations issue stock to raise money. To see how this works, let's imagine you have just invented and patented a new mousetrap, one that will trap a mouse, vaporize it and transport its remains to Mars. You know these will be a big seller if you can just make them in large quantities. You want to start a new company, which you are going to call "Mickey Mousetrap, Inc." But you need money; that is, you need some capital funds in order to buy some capital goods.

One way to get it would be to go to a bank and borrow some money. But the bank might have some doubts about how well your new mousetrap is going to work. And they are going to want to know a lot about your personal financial situation. And, most likely, they will want some collateral to secure your investment. That means you may have to put up your house, or any other assets you own, as security for a bank loan. You don't want to do that, so, instead, you decide to start your own corporation and sell shares in it to outside investors.

To do that, you have to file papers with the state you reside in to incorporate your company and pay a small fee. Now you are ready to sell shares in an initial public offering (IPO). Let's say you need to raise $1,000,000 to launch this business. One way to approach this would be to find ten people each with $100,000 to invest as **venture capitalists**. Each of them would then own ten percent of your company, but you wouldn't own any of it. So, most likely, you will keep some of the stock for yourself and sell the rest, or you might invest some of your own money. Either way, you want to retain some ownership yourself, or none of this would make any sense. Let's say you invest $500,000 of your own money, which gives you half ownership, and want to sell the rest to investors. Now you have a strategy problem.

 Key Concept: Venture capitalists are investors who focus on investing in new, often risky, business ventures.

If you issue 10 shares of stock at $100,000 and buy five shares yourself, then you have to find five investors to put up $100,000 each, and they would each own 10 percent of the company. Finding five investors to put $100,000 each into a new mousetrap company would not be easy, so instead you would probably decide to issue more shares at a lower price, say 10,000 shares at $100 each, and buy 5,000 yourself. Now your sales job is easier because a lot more people would be willing to buy smaller amounts of the stock at the lower price.

Let's say you sell 10,000 shares at $100 each. Each share of stock then represents a small percentage of ownership in the company. Once the stock is issued and sold you have raised the money you need to launch the company, but now you have some problems—bosses to contend with.

Establishing a Board of Directors

With 5,000 shares held internally, that is, by you as an "insider," there are 5,000 shares held by the public, or what is called "floating" in the market. The owners of the floating shares will most likely not be interested in managing the company directly. Instead, they will want to elect a board of directors to oversee its operations.

In a small company, a Board of Directors is generally made up of stockholders who have a vote on the board proportional to the number of shares they own. They will not want to participate directly in the day-to-day management of the company either. Instead, they will most likely elect a Chairman of the Board to perform that function, and he or she will probably appoint a president as General Manager or Chief Executive Officer (CEO) of the company. Under normal circumstances, since you want to manage the company (and own 50 percent of it), you would be named president. In that role you would be expected to report to the Chairman of the Board on a regular basis, and to the entire board at monthly or quarterly meetings.

Dividends and Retained Earnings

Once your company is up and running and (let's assume) profitable then you have to contend with the question of what to do with the profits. Stockholders expect to be paid **dividends**, a percentage return on their investment. But you also need to keep some of the profits as **retained earnings**, to be reinvested in the company to make it grow and expand. The stockholders also have an interest in some of the profits being plowed back into the company because they want to see the value of their stock *appreciate*, that is, increase in value over time. Therefore, you and the board have a strategy decision to make.

Key Concept: Dividends are that portion of corporate profits distributed to stockholders.

Key Concept: Retained earnings are that portion of profits retained for reinvestment in the corporation for expansion.

Normally, but not always, a well-run, prospering company will distribute part of its net earnings (above costs) as dividends and retain part for reinvestment. For example, let's assume that your company has earned a $10,000 profit over the past year, and that you (as CEO) and the board have decided that it would be prudent to retain half of it ($5,000) as undistributed corporate profits for reinvestment. The other half ($5,000) is to be distributed to shareholders as dividends. What will each shareholder receive?

Because there are 10,000 shares outstanding, a $5,000 distribution means each share of stock is valued at $.50 per share (10,000/$5,000). An investor who owns 2,000 shares is paid $1,000 ($.50 x 2,000) in dividends. Note also that as the owner of 50 percent of the company—with 5,000 shares—you also receive a dividend of $2,500 ($.50 x 5,000). This is in addition to any salary you receive as Chief Executive Officer, which is part of the company's operating expenses.

What we have just seen here is a classic, albeit somewhat oversimplified, example of how capitalism works. As an entrepreneur, you developed a new product, patented it, started your own company, incorporated it, invested part of your own money in it, and issued and sold stock to raise the additional capital you needed to get the company going. After the stock was sold you established a Board of Directors, which elected a Chairman. The board appointed you as Chief Executive Officer to manage the company and you retained fifty-percent ownership. This was your original goal, and if the company is successful at producing and selling the new mousetraps you will also be successful. You have become a capitalist, an entrepreneur who has been able to combine the factors of production: land, labor, and capital with your managerial skills and your willingness to take a risk to start a new company—and you share in the profits. Of course, if the company had failed you would have shared—in a big way—in the losses. That's how capitalism works.

Interestingly, just because you have started a new company that seems to be successful, your problems are not over. In addition to dealing with the day-to-day managerial problems of running the company, and dealing with the Board of Directors and the stockholders, you have to deal with the **Securities and Exchange Commission** (SEC), the governmental agency that watches over publicly owned companies. That means, among other things, you have to file financial reports, including an annual report.

 Key Concept: The Securities and Exchange Commission is the governmental agency charged with overseeing and regulating the financial markets.

The Annual Report

You and the board will also need to prepare an annual report, which summarizes the prior year's operations, projects future developments, and provides a detailed statement of the company's financial position. This report must be presented at an annual meeting to which all stockholders are invited to attend. Those who can't attend personally will be asked to sign a proxy, giving their vote to another stockholder or, more likely, to a member of the Board of Directors who will vote in their interest should there be an important issue to be approved by the stockholders.

HOW TO READ FINANCIAL REPORTS

Every year, a publicly owned company is required to file with the Securities and Exchange Commission a detailed accounting of its financial condition, including information about key personnel and important changes in the company's business. Most investors don't see this report, (a "10-K" report), but rather the annual report, which the company mails to stockholders. The annual report is less detailed than the 10-K, but it contains key information, which is what most investors are looking for. Another key document is the form "10-Q," or quarterly report. This gives a summary of a company's performance during its most recent quarter. Also, a form "8-K" must be filed with the SEC within 15 days of any events or changes in a business that are of great importance to shareholders. Many other documents must also be filed, but the 10-K, the 8-K, and the annual report are the most important.

Many libraries carry books that summarize financial information on companies making comparisons among them easy. For example, *Value Line Investment Survey* gives one-page summaries on thousands of companies and can be found in many libraries, or individual investors can subscribe.

The Income Statement

Probably the most important single figure we can find from financial documents is how much money the company we're analyzing is making or losing—the so-called "bottom line." It's called the bottom line because it is generally the last line in the first financial statement we'll look at, the **income statement**. Because a company's stock price is based on its ability to make money for investors in the future, and because an income statement records the company's historical record of making money, knowing your way around an income statement is crucial. An income statement is also one of the simplest financial statements to read: it lists all the money made during a certain period, and deducts the expenses required to make it. What's left is either a profit (called net income or net earnings) or a loss.

 Key Concept: A company's income statement compares total income to total expenses. The difference between the two is net earnings or net profit—the so-called "bottom line."

Suppose you're in college and you start a clothing business for students at your school. In a school year you sold $60,000 worth of custom-printed sweatshirts, at an average price of $20 per shirt. You bought the shirts from a wholesaler for $10 each, then you paid a graphic artist to come up with designs, paid a printer to print the designs on the sweatshirts, paid friends to sell the shirts, and paid the bank interest on a loan you took out to buy the shirts initially.

At year's end, your net earnings were $12,000. Suppose you had raised money to start your business by selling stock. Let's say you kicked in $600 and others kicked in $600, buying 600 shares you sold for $1 each. To find out how much money you would have made for each share, (called "earnings per share"), you simply divide the net earnings by the number of shares ($12,000/ 1,200 = $10). Does this mean that everyone who holds a share of stock gets

---

Figure 2-1 **SWEATSHIRT, INC. STATEMENT OF INCOME**

INCOME STATEMENT
December 31, 1995

Sales	$	60,000
Cost of Goods Sold	$	35,000
Gross Profit	$	25,000
Selling, General and Administrative Expenses	$	5,000
Interest Expense	$	2,000
Income Taxes	$	6,000
Net Earnings	$	12,000
Earnings Per Share	$	10

---

paid $10? Not necessarily. As we have seen, the company can decide whether it wants to pay out some or all of the profits. This payout is the dividend. The money kept in the company is called retained earnings. Those retained earnings will be invested to help the company grow even larger.

Let's suppose that half of the net earnings will be paid out in dividends and see how that shows up on Sweatshirt, Inc.'s income statement (Figure 2-1). This income statement illustrates how all the money you brought in is listed first. Then each line of **expenses** chips away at our pile of money until—hopefully—there is profit left by the bottom line. Typical expenses range from salaries paid to employees, to minor expenses such as the cost of stamps used to send letters and the cost of the paper used to write a letter. Advertising is also an expense, as is the rent you pay for the offices where you conduct your business.

 Key Concept: Expenses are the cost of materials and services used up in the course of getting revenue. Also called the "cost of doing business."

Figure 2-2 **SWEATSHIRT, INC. BALANCE SHEET**

BALANCE SHEET
December 31, 1995

Assets		Liabilities	
Cash	$ 3,000	Notes Payable	$ 2,000
Accounts Receivable (money owed us)	$ 3,000	Accounts Payable (money we owe others)	$ 1,988
Supplies	$ 2,000	Stockholder's Equity:	
Embossing Equipment	$ 2,000	Common Stock	$ 12
		Retained Earnings	$ 6,000
			$ 6,012
Total Assets	$10,000	Total Liabilities and Stockholder's Equity	$10,000

By comparing income statements from year to year, and from company to company in the same industry, we can determine whether the company is improving steadily, erratically, or not at all. Say, for example, our sweatshirt company had the same sales in the next year, but we paid more for advertising, so profits dropped. Obviously advertising didn't increase sales, so our new advertising campaign actually hurt our profits—a poor business decision. Likewise, if a company's expenses increase while sales remain the same, it could be the sign of poor management.

The Balance Sheet

Another major financial statement that all companies must prepare is the **balance sheet**. The balance sheet shows what a business owns, what a business owes, and what's left over at a certain point in time. This differs from an income statement, which records the sales and expenses over a period of time. A balance sheet is divided into two parts, which, when added up, must be the same, or balance. A balance sheet can tell an investor a great deal about the financial health of the company. Is the company too far in debt? Does it have enough cash to pay its bills? These are important questions for investors.

Key Concept: A company's balance sheet shows what it owns compared to what it owes.

In Figure 2-2, the balance sheet of Sweatshirt Inc., we see that at the end of the year the company has $3,000 in the bank, is expecting to collect $3,000 from customers (accounts receivable), has $2,000 in unprinted sweatshirts and other supplies, and has a machine for putting designs on sweatshirts worth $2,000. Together, these make up the company's assets. On the other side of the balance sheet, the company owes the bank $2,000, and owes the sweatshirt supplier $1,988 (accounts payable). The company also has $6,000 in retained earnings—it made $12,000 in its first year, paid $6,000 out in dividends and kept the rest—and is recording the value of its stock at $12. This doesn't reflect the true value of the stock but is simply the stock recorded at par value, in this case a penny a share.

Using Ratios

To help summarize data about profitability, we can use ratios, which show relationships between sales, stock prices, and earnings. For example, by dividing a company's net income by its sales, we get a measure of what percent of a company's sales ends up as profits, called **return on sales**.

 Key Concept: Return on sales = net income divided by sales.

To compare profits to a company's stock price, we divide earnings per share by price per share, called the **price-earnings ratio**, or simply P/E. If there are two companies in the business, Company A with earnings of $4 per share and a stock price of $40 per share, and Company B with earnings of $2 per share and a stock price of $14 per share, which would you buy? Using the price/earnings ratio as a guide, Company A has a P/E of 10 (40/4), while company B has a P/E of 7 (14/2). Therefore, Company B is cheaper, because it's earning you more money for your investment dollar than Company A. So it would seem that, all things being equal, you should buy company B. However, for example, if company B has a major lawsuit against it, or has just had its main factory destroyed by fire, or if something else has happened that would cause demand for its stock to drop, and therefore its price, it might not be such a bargain after all. This is why a company must be thoroughly investigated before investing in it. Price/ earnings ratios don't always tell the whole story. Also, different industries have different price and earnings structures, so P/E's are most useful comparing corporations in the same line of business —apples-to-apples, as it were.

Key Concept: A price-earnings ratio is a company's current stock price divided by its current estimated earnings per share.

Debt Ratios

While examining a company's balance sheet, investors are often interested in the company's ability to pay its bills—its *current debt ratio*. This measure compares the company's current assets, or money readily available (cash, investments, accounts receivable), with current liabilities, or bills it must soon pay. This current ratio divides a company's current assets by its current liabilities. If a company has twice as much short-term funds as it has short-term bills—a current ratio of two—it is generally thought to have good bill-paying ability. In Sweatshirt Inc.'s case, for example, it has $6,000 in current assets and about $4,000 in current liabilities, for a current debt ratio of 1.5 ($6,000/$4,000 = 1.5).

Another important ratio that uses balance sheet figures is the *equity ratio*, calculated by the total stockholders' equity divided by the company's total assets. This ratio measures the percentage of assets matched by stockholders' equity, and shows how much of the company's assets are financed by debt, as opposed to those owned outright by the company. Another way of saying this is how much "leverage" a company is using. **Financial leverage** is the degree to which a company borrows against its assets. Leverage is used to describe many different financial situations. In the most basic sense, leverage simply means using what you have to get more. It's important to remember, however, that using leverage almost always means adding some risk to a situation.

 Key Concept: Financial leverage is how much a company is borrowing in relation to its equity.

Another measure of leverage is a company's *debt ratio*, or total assets divided by total liabilities. The higher the debt ratio, the more money a company has borrowed relative to its assets. Of course, higher debt means more interest expense must be paid, increasing the chance the company won't be able to pay its debts and will go out of business if earnings decline. But usually a prudent amount of debt adds to the earnings power of a company without significantly increasing risk if the money borrowed is invested properly.

In the best case, a company makes a higher return investing the money it borrowed versus the interest it must pay on the money borrowed. For example, if a company earns 25 percent on the assets it has and can borrow money at 10 percent, it makes 15 percent on the money it borrows. Note, however, that highly leveraged companies represent higher risk to investors, and smart investors take this factor into account.

Other popular ratios use figures from both the income statement and balance sheet. *Return on assets* (ROA) is calculated by dividing net income by assets and shows how efficiently a company uses its assets. Take, for example, two companies in the same industry. If Company A has an ROA of 15, and Company B has an ROA of 5, we know that Company A squeezes three times more profits out of its assets as Company B. A similar ratio is *return on stockholders' equity*, which divides net income by stockholders' equity.

All of these ratios, which can be calculated from a company's income statement and balance sheet, are important measures of a company's financial health. At the least, they provide company analysts and potential investors with useful information to assess a company as a potential investment opportunity.

WHO CARES ABOUT STOCK PRICES?

Interestingly, once stock has been issued and the company has received the capital funds it needs for expansion or modernization, the market price of its stock doesn't follow the day-to-day operations of the company, although, over time, the company's stock price rises and falls with its success. This is what has led some to suggest that the stock market is nothing more than a giant casino where players gamble to win or lose without any connection to the real world of business or the economy.

In one sense this is true, but, in another it is not. To see why, let's consider the two kinds of stock purchases. In one, we simply buy some stock in an existing company. Our purchase has virtually no effect on the price of the company's stock or on its fortunes. We are just gambling in the stock market casino that the stocks will turn out to be a good investment from which we can make some money. And, as in a casino, we could also lose.

In the example of Mickey Mousetrap, Inc., if we had bought some of the newly issued stock we were certainly gambling, but we were also investing in the company in a more direct way. We were providing the company with the capital it needed to launch a new business which, among other things, helped a new product come into being and created new jobs. This is quite different from simply buying an existing "floating" stock.

It is also important to recognize that investors are not alone in caring about stock prices. The management of a corporation with outstanding stock also has an interest in what happens to the price of its stock. There are several reasons. One is that if a company's stock price is increasing, then the public *perceives* that it is doing well, making it easier for it to raise additional funds if needed. Another reason managers care about stock prices is that in virtually all cases the managers of a corporation own a portion of the outstanding stock. Recall, for example, that as the CEO of Mickey Mousetrap, Inc., you own fifty percent of the outstanding stock. When the price of the stock increases, the management gains as much or more than the other stockholders. Finally, managers have to answer to their stockholders. If the company is not doing well and its stock price is falling, the stockholders may demand an explanation—if not a replacement in management.

SUMMARY

- ✓ Capitalism is a system of economic organization in which business enterprises are owned by private individuals, as opposed to being owned by the government.
- ✓ Individuals who are willing to invest their money in new businesses and bear the risk of failure are called entrepreneurs.
- ✓ There are three basic forms of business organization, each depending upon the system by which they are owned.
- ✓ Sole proprietorships are owned by one individual who bears total responsibility for running the business.
- ✓ Partnerships involve two or more owners who are responsible for the business.
- ✓ Corporations operate as if they were an individual but are owned by their stockholders who appoint management.
- ✓ Stocks represent a small portion of ownership in a corporation and all of its assets.
- ✓ Successful corporations usually share part of their earnings with stockholders in the form of dividends.
- ✓ Corporations are required by the Securities and Exchange Commission to file detailed financial reports each year. These include annual reports, 10k reports, income statements, and balance sheets.
- ✓ One good measure of a corporation's financial viability is its price/earnings ratio—the ratio of its current stock share price to its estimated earnings per share.
- ✓ Other important ratios include current debt ratios, equity ratios, and return on assets.

✓ Stock prices are important to investors who expect to earn dividends as well as capital gains through increases in the price of the stocks they own. Managers share in that expectation to the extent that they also own stock in the corporations they manage.

NEW VOCABULARY

entrepreneurship
sole proprietorships
partnerships
corporations
capital
stocks
dividends
retained earnings

Securities and Exchange
  Commission
financial reports
income statements
balance sheets
expenses
price/earnings ratios
debt ratios

QUESTIONS FOR REVIEW

1. What are the four things required to produce anything?
2. What is meant by the word entrepreneurship?
3. What is the difference between a sole proprietorship, a partnership, and a corporation?
4. How do you distinguish between real capital and financial capital?
5. What is a stock?
6. What does it mean to own stock in a corporation?
7. What is a venture capitalist?
8. What is the difference between dividends and retained earnings?
9. What does an income statement tell you about a corporation's financial situation?
10. What is meant by the term price/earnings ratio?

Chapter 3

THE ECONOMICS OF ACCOUNTING*

LEARNING OBJECTIVES

In this chapter we take a look at the basics of accounting with emphasis on:
- ✓ What is accounting?
- ✓ The role accounting plays in our economy.
- ✓ How an accounting system functions.
- ✓ The meaning of basic accounting terms.
- ✓ What the major financial statements produced with accounting information tell us.
- ✓ How to record basic accounting data and then use it to generate information that is useful in the decision-making process.
- ✓ The construction of two major financial statements: the balance sheet and income statement.

INTRODUCTION

What is Accounting?

Accounting is an information system designed to record, organize, present, and analyze economic activity. The information generated by an accounting system is used as the basis for making decisions of primarily a financial nature.

When people think of accounting, an image usually comes to mind of dull "bean counters" scribbling away at dusty ledgers or pecking figures into a computer keyboard, boring people crunching boring numbers that have little to do with the real concerns of flesh-and-blood human beings. However, if we

---

* Professor Craig Hovey of Keuka College contributed this chapter.

pause to take a look at what is really going on we quickly see that this is not exactly what accounting really means. Accounting does indeed rely on numbers to record data and communicate information, and these numbers are stated in terms of monetary units (dollars, yen, marks, and so on), but we must bear in mind what these represent.

In a broad sense these numbers are used to record some of the millions of exchanges taking place in our country every day that form the basis of our economy: people exchanging their labor for a salary they then exchange for food and shelter; the government collecting taxes to pay for the provision of services to its citizens, companies exchanging their goods and services for dollars they go on to trade for more raw materials and human resources to be made into something new with the intention of exchanging it for yet more dollars; and the list goes on. *In essence, an accounting system uses the language of money to tell us about the financial results of a set of human actions.*

Because our economy is so vast and diverse it would be impossible for one accounting system to keep track of everything going on in it. Rather, individual accounting systems are employed to record the transactions that concern particular entities, whether a large corporation, a small family-run business, or a governmental unit. Although there is wide variety in how these different concerns function, an accounting system can be adapted to each of them to effectively track the economic activities that comprise the business at hand.

WHAT ACCOUNTING INFORMATION TELLS US

To put it simply, accounting information lets us know what we own; what we owe; what is left over after our debts are paid; the resources that flowed in during a particular period, and the resources sacrificed to generate that inflow. Think of an accounting system as a special kind of camera that uses units of money to paint a financial picture of where an entity is at a particular point in time, while also documenting the steps taken to get there.

In the United States businesses and consumers operate in a relatively free market economy. In this capitalistic system we assume businesses and individuals operate out of the profit motive, which means we all want to become better off as the result of our efforts.

The reason accounting measures profit and wealth in dollars is not because accountants are particularly money hungry, but rather, since wealth is too subjective a term to nail down to everybody's satisfaction, we use money because it is a common standard of measurement we can agree on. Obviously, using money as a measure and way of communication means that there are many things accounting systems cannot tell us, but at the same time we have the advantage of using a language capable of providing plenty of valuable information within its scope.

The next thing to look at is how we go about making ourselves better off. Our economy is based on mutual exchanges, meaning you can trade something you have that somebody else wants (your labor for example) for something you want (the money to pay rent and buy CD's). The catch is that resources (what people have to exchange) are limited. This means that in order to improve your well-being to the maximum extent possible you must trade your resources carefully to get the most possible in exchange for them. After all, if you squander resources (like time, talent, and money) on things that do not give you much in return you obviously will be worse off as a result. However, by using these same resources wisely you can trade your way into a better future. This is the essence of earning profits and increasing wealth.

Every time you spend resources to do one thing it means those same resources are no longer available for any other alternatives. For example, if you have to take an important test tomorrow morning and have only three free hours available tonight, chances are studying will be the best use of your time. If you instead spend those hours watching television, you will waste the chance to be prepared for the test and will not perform as well. The cost of watching TV can be measured as the points you lost on the exam because you chose not to study.

The opportunity cost (the value of the possible choices not taken), as we saw in Chapter 1, should never exceed the value of the choice that is made. In accounting, as in life, opportunity cost is a valuable tool to use as a guide in decision making.

Even though an accounting system will not keep specific track of opportunity costs, it does tell you how well, or poorly, you chose to use your resources. Put yourself in the position of one who has invested savings, time, talent, and energy in a new business. Because you are risking all these resources on an enterprise that probably didn't come with any guarantees of success, you want to see it grow and prosper, to profit in ways that reward you for all that hard work, sacrifice, and risk. If you are successful, your accounting system will document it by showing that your business has been able to grow and profit by taking in more (in the form of sales for example) than was spent to produce those sales (expenses like wages, rent, materials, and so on).

This means you exchanged the resources at your command for resources of greater value to you (usually in the form of money). On the other hand, if your business shrinks and shows a loss by taking in less than was spent, your accounting system will also document the lack of success. Either way, valuable information is provided, which is essential to making decisions about what opportunities to pursue in the future.

ACCOUNTING TERMINOLOGY

When accountants talk about the resources sacrificed with the goal of making a profit they refer to them as **expenses**, meaning what you have to give up, or pay, in dollar terms in order to operate your business. Expenses include spending on things like salaries, utilities, cost of goods sold, and depreciation (wearing out things like buildings and equipment), all necessary expenditures to run a business.

Key Concept: Expenses are the dollar value of those resources sacrificed to generate revenues.

The opposite of expenses is what you receive in exchange for sacrificed resources, or **revenues**, which occur when you make sales, earn commissions, and provide services. Revenues are extremely important because they represent an incoming stream of resources needed to operate your business. Revenues are used to pay the bills, pay for further investment in the business, pay taxes to the government, and, most important, to pay yourself as the owner of the business.

Key Concept: Revenues are the dollar value of the resources flowing in as the result of an exchange.

When revenues exceed expenses the difference is referred to as **profit**. This means you had more coming in than going out, which is what you want to see happen. When revenues are lower than expenses the difference is referred to as a loss: less came in than went out, which, obviously, you want to avoid.

Key Concept: When revenues exceed expenses the business earns a profit. If expenses exceed revenues the business suffers a loss.

Assets are the things a business owns. They can include land, buildings, equipment, cash, accounts receivable, and inventory; the list will vary depending on the business. Entrepreneurs invest in the assets that are necessary to the operation of their enterprise with the goal of using them to increase their well-being, or wealth, by earning profits, but that doesn't happen overnight.

Key Concept: Assets are what a business owns.

Soon after investment in the necessary assets, the business will start using them up in the form of expenses exchanged with others in the effort to earn revenue in return. For example, the inventory purchased gets sold, the equipment recently installed is run, and the new building is utilized. As portions of assets are used they are turned into expenses just as costs like salaries and supplies are. If you run a car dealership and sell a car you paid $10,000 for to a customer for $15,000, the $10,000 cost of the car is an expense—what you had to sacrifice in order to gain a sale (earn revenue) of $15,000 and a profit on the sale of $5,000 ($15,000–$10,000). Put differently, you purchased an asset for $10,000 and sold it for $15,000.

Some long-term assets, like buildings and equipment, are used up over a period of years instead of being exchanged during one particular year. In these cases accountants depreciate them. **Depreciation** refers to the practice of estimating the portion of an asset's value that is used up each year and then showing it as an expense so you can see how much of an asset's worth was sacrificed in a particular year to earn revenue.

Key Concept: Depreciation represents an estimate of the portion of a long-term asset's value that is used up in one particular period.

Now let's say that all this talk of revenues, expenses, and profits has gotten you so excited that you have decided to go out and open up a pizza shop and make your fortune. You begin by figuring out what the assets are that you must invest in before opening for business. In this case we'll assume these include equipment (ovens and refrigerators), a building, and materials for making the pizza (cheese, sauce, dough, and so on). But, unless you happen to be independently wealthy, chances are you will not have enough money in your piggy bank to buy everything you need. Does this mean you have to wait until you've been able to save enough? No. You can do what most businesses do: borrow other people's money.

Any resource borrowed, which is then used to finance the purchase of assets, is called a **liability**. A liability is something you owe that must be paid back at some point in the future. Almost anything you borrow comes along with an interest charge, the cost of having the use of that resource, that must also be paid back along with whatever was borrowed. So when you borrow funds to invest in your business you should be sure that you will be able to use them in a way that allows you to earn enough in the future to cover the cost of repaying the liability, meeting the obligation for interest, and, let's not forget, have enough left over to compensate yourself for taking on all the risks and headaches of operating a business.

Key Concept: Liabilities are what a business owes.

The kinds of liabilities you would use to finance the investment in your business could include a mortgage to purchase the building, a loan for buying the equipment, and short-term credit to order the materials. You will pay off the bigger debts, like the mortgage and loan, in monthly installments over a period of years, and each payment will include an interest charge along with a portion of the principle borrowed. The short-term debts you ran up using credit will probably be paid off on a monthly basis or over a period of months, like a charge card.

Of course, borrowing is not the only way to raise money for your business. You can also (as we saw in the previous chapter) bring in additional financing by selling stock to people interested in investing in the business. A person who buys a company's stock becomes a part owner of that business. The total value of the owner's interest in a business is called **equity**. Equity refers to the total invested by the owners, (personal funds put into the business or the amount of stock purchased), plus any earnings retained by the business. Equity is also what is left over after you subtract liabilities (what you owe) from your assets (what you own).

 Key Concept: Equity is the value of the owner's stake in a business.

Many businesses finance their asset acquisitions with a mix of liabilities and equities. This is often done in stages as the business grows. For example, you might be able to pay for everything you need out of your own pocket when your business first starts up, so the amount of your money invested represents the total equity of the business. If you later wish to expand but cannot afford the cost of the new assets necessary to do so, you can borrow money through bank loans or you can issue bonds, which would serve the same function as a loan. You would pay interest over a period of years then repay the principle when the bonds mature. Then, in order to expand again, you might sell shares of stock on the open market to interested investors who now become owners along with you.[1]

When liabilities, such as loans, are used for financing, the principal and interest must be repaid sooner or later. But, when equity is used (using personal resources or selling stock), the funds do not need to be paid back because they came from the owners of the business. Given this, a natural

---

[1] The process of starting a company and issuing stock is treated in more detail in the Durell Teaching Kit entitled *DEMYSTIFYING THE STOCK MARKET.*

assumption is that one should only raise money through selling stock since it doesn't ever have to be paid back. That may be true, but the buyers of stock become owners and will want a say in how things are run, and they may want a share of the business's earnings paid out to them in the form of **dividends**. However, stockholders can make money from their investment even when dividends are not paid if the stock appreciates in market value.

 Key Concept: Dividends are distributions of earnings to the stockholders of a business.

You now know that a good accounting system shows you what you have invested in (assets); where you got the resources to do that from (liabilities and equity); what portion of assets you sacrificed; plus other costs of operations in the current period (expenses); what you were able to exchange the resources sacrificed for (revenue); and how much better (profit) or worse (loss) off you are as a result of your entrepreneurial activities.

THE ACCOUNTING SYSTEM

Because investment in assets can only be financed with liabilities and/or equity it is possible to state the relationship between them in what is known as the accounting equation:

Liabilities + Owner's Equity = Assets,

which can also be written like this:

Assets – Liabilities = Equity

Since these relationships must always exist, an accounting system is by definition always self-balancing. Further, every time data is recorded in an accounting system, the individual entries must always balance, and the entire system must balance after each change is made—no matter how many occur. This is a great strength because it allows the user of a system to track where resources are, or where they have gone, and how they are being utilized.

In an accounting system, every economic event recorded will affect at least one, and possibly all three, of the categories listed above, but no matter how great the effect the accounting equation will always hold (this will become more evident shortly). The effects of entries will be to either cause increases or decreases in the dollar amounts listed as assets, liabilities, and equity. Accountants have specific names for these increases and decreases:

Debits: These are used to increase asset accounts or decrease liability and equity accounts.

Credits: These are used to decrease asset accounts or increase liability and equity accounts.

It is important to remember that debits and credits affect assets the opposite of how they affect liabilities and equity.

When an economic event is initially recorded in dollars and cents using debits and credits, this is called a **journal entry**. A journal entry is merely a listing of the accounts and the debits and credits that are used to tell us about a particular transaction. The important thing to remember is that both debits and credits must be present in every journal entry and also that the total dollar amount of debits and the total dollar amount of credits must always be the same. By adhering to these rules every journal entry will balance and the accounting system as a whole will remain in balance after incorporating the new information. If the accounting equation doesn't work out right at any time, we know an error has been made and can go back through our records to check for the mistake.

 Key Concept: A journal entry uses debits and credits to show the changes in asset, liability, or equity accounts as the result of an economic event.

In order to keep track of things and record them clearly it is common practice for debits to be on the left side of a journal entry with credits on the right, like this:

Debit	*$$$$*	
Credit		*$$$$*

By convention there is also a short explanation given below each entry showing why it was entered.

As you can imagine, during the course of most business operations many, many economic events are recorded in the form of journal entries. All of these are initially recorded in one place, called the general journal. Because this can get pretty unwieldy and make it difficult to find a particular entry, **ledgers** are used to group together transactions of a similar nature in one place by transferring (called posting) information from the general journal to a particular ledger. Typically an accountant will have separate ledgers for accounts: things like cash, inventory, accounts payable, and so on. These provide valuable records of activity in specific areas, as opposed to just a listing of everything going on like we see in the general journal. So, for example, if you want to get an idea of how you are doing at collecting money from customers who owe you, you can go right to the accounts receivable ledger.

 Key Concept: Ledgers serve to group together all the changes in a particular account in one place.

Journal entries are entered over periods of time (usually months, quarters and years) and then posted to ledgers at regular intervals during that time. The ledgers' entries are totaled up and used to produce different sets of *financial statements* that provide specific information about what happened over a specific period. These statements are usually produced at least annually but are commonly done on a quarterly and monthly basis too. The most common financial statements (described below) are developed for different purposes, but they all rely on the same economic information, which originates in the journal entries.

 Key Concept: Financial statements are used to provide specific information about a business's status on a particular date and activities during a specific period

- **Balance Sheet:** Lists the total assets, liabilities, and owner's equity of an enterprise at a particular point in time, usually the end of a year. Often the balance sheets for more than one year will be shown together to illustrate the changes that took place over time.

- **Income Statement:** Shows the revenues earned and expenses incurred by an enterprise during a period of time. Expenses are subtracted from revenues to show the income for the period shown. This income can be either positive (a profit) or negative (a loss).

- **Cash Flow:** Shows the sources of all cash flows into and out of the business. For example, a cash flow statement could tell us about the cash raised through the sales of stocks and bonds (inflow) and what assets were purchased with them (outflow).

- **Owner's Equity:** Displays the beginning balances in the stock accounts and retained earnings and lists the additions and subtractions to these during the course of a financial period. These can include additional sales of stock, net income, and dividends declared or paid out.

ACCOUNTING ILLUSTRATED

As opposed to some sciences, such as economics, accounting has always been a very practically oriented discipline, where the connection between theory and application is quite close. As such, the best way to understand how an accounting system works is to walk through what is done in one over a period of time, and that's just what we'll do now. For continuity we will use the example of opening a pizza shop introduced earlier and use the information generated from its first year of business to illustrate the accounting principles we have introduced so far. Our example will begin by listing the information used to generate journal entries, constructing the entries, organizing the information in the appropriate accounts, and then producing a set of financial statements.

Below is a list of economic events that occur during our first year in the pizza business. Read through them first, then follow how they are treated in the steps below.

A) We invest $60,000 of our own savings in the business.

B) We take out a loan from the bank of $40,000.

C) Ovens are purchased for $30,000.

D) Rent of $15,000 is paid for the year.

E) We pay $55,000 for a building.

F) $14,000 of pizza ingredients are purchased on credit.

G) $12,000 of pizza ingredients are used up in order to make pizzas we sell for $100,000.

H) Salaries of $45,000 are paid to the employees.

I) The ovens and equipment are depreciated by $2,000.

J) We repay $5,000 of the loan.

K) $11,000 of the credit account is paid off.

L) Interest of $1,000 is paid.

M) We, reluctantly, pay taxes of $2,000.

STEP ONE: JOURNAL ENTRIES

Here we will record the events from above in our general journal, the same letters are used so we can refer back and forth if necessary. As you read the entries think about why the amounts go where they are put. Remember: debits, offset to the left, are used to signify an increase in an asset account or a decrease in liabilities or equity. Credits, offset to the right, are used to signify a decrease in an asset account or an increase in liabilities or equity. Total debits and total credits will always be equal.

GENERAL JOURNAL

JOURNAL ENTRY		DEBITS	CREDITS
A)	Cash	60,000	
	Owner's Equity		60,000
B)	Cash	40,000	
	Long-term Debt		40,000
C)	Ovens	30,000	
	Cash		30,000
D)	Rent Expense	15,000	
	Cash		15,000
E)	Building	55,000	
	Cash		55,000
F)	Ingredients Inventory	14,000	
	Accounts Payable		14,000
G)	Cash	100,000	
	Cost of Goods Sold	12,000	
	Inventory		12,000
	Sales Revenue		100,000
H)	Salary Expense	45,000	
	Cash		45,000
I)	Depreciation Expense	2,000	
	Accumulated Depreciation		2,000
J)	Long-term Debt	5,000	
	Cash		5,000
K)	Account Payable	11,000	
	Cash		11,000
L)	Interest Expense	1,000	
	Cash		1,000
M)	Tax Expense	2,000	
	Cash		2,000

STEP TWO: LEDGER ACCOUNTS

Clearly, trying to keep track of everything that happens using only a general journal gets difficult if more than a few things happen in a given period. In many businesses there may be millions of different transactions to record, which is why information is usually posted (transferred) from the general journal to specific ledgers. Below, the ledgers are grouped together under headings depending on what category they fit into: assets (what we own), liabilities (what we owe), or equity (the owner's interest). Please note that revenues and expenses are shown in the retained earnings account of owner's equity: this is because inflows of resources (revenues) increase the wealth of the owners and outflows of resources (expenses) reduce the wealth of the owners. As you can see, the practice of grouping similar transactions together makes it much easier to keep an eye on them.

A simplified form of ledger called a T-account is used below. As with the journal entries, debits go on the left and credits on the right. We will continue to use the original letters from the journal entries so you can continue keeping track of where things are being put, and why. Notice that totals for the period for each ledger account are arrived at by combining the debits and credits and performing simple subtraction.

ASSETS

INGREDIENTS

CASH		INVENTORY		OVENS	
Debits	Credits	Debits	Credits	Debits	Credits
a) 60,000		f) 14,000		c) 30,000	
b) 40,000			g) 12,000		
	c) 30,000				
	d) 15,000				
	e) 55,000				
	g) 100,000				
	h) 45,000				
	j) 5,000				
	k) 11,000				
	l) 1,000				
	m) 2,000				
$36,000		$2,000		$30,000	

ACCUMULATED

BUILDING	DEPRECIATION
e) 55,000	J) 2,000
$55,000	$2,000

Total Assets: $121,000.

This total is obtained by adding up the balances of all the asset accounts at the end of our accounting period. These individual totals tell us how much of each asset we have on hand, the total combines them into one number. Notice that all but one asset account have debit balances, which means we have positive quantities of assets. The exception is accumulated depreciation, which serves to reduce our assets by the amount of depreciation taken (value of long-term assets used up). So here's how we arrived at total assets: Cash of $36,000 + Ingredients of $2,000 + Ovens of $30,000 + Building of $55,000—depreciation on Ovens & Building of $2,000 = **$121,000.**

LIABILITIES

ACCOUNTS PAYABLE	LONG TERM DEBT
f) 14,000	b) 40,000
m) 11,000	J) 5,000
$3,000	$35,000

Total Liabilities: $38,000.

As with assets, the individual totals tell us where the account stands at the end of the period, the final total combines all of them. The reason for credit balances in the liability accounts is that here they indicate a positive balance, which represents what we still owe. The total shows: Accounts Payable of $3,000 + Long-term Debt of $35,000 = **$38,000.**

OWNER'S EQUITY

OWNER'S CAPITAL		RETAINED EARNINGS	
	a) 60,000	d) 15,000	
		g) 12,000	g) 100,000
		h) 45,000	
		i) 2,000	
		l) 1,000	
		m) 2,000	
	$60,000		$23,000

Total Owner's Equity: $83,000.

The owner's capital account shows the initial investment. If this were a firm that sold stock, the listings for stockholders' equity would tell us what those owners had invested in the company. Retained earnings let us know how much of our earnings are being kept in the business. In this case, since it's a new enterprise, there were no earnings to begin with, but we were able to finish the year with $23,000 after we were through paying expenses. We arrived at the total by adding Owner's Capital of $60,000 + Retained Earnings of $23,000 = **$83,000**.

As you'll see, we finished with our accounting system in balance, as the basic accounting requires. To see why, let's take our totals and plug the numbers in:

$$LIABILITIES + EQUITY = ASSETS$$
$$\$38,000 + \$83,000 = \$121,000$$

or

$$ASSETS - LIABILITIES = EQUITY$$
$$\$121,000 - \$38,000 = \$83,000$$

STEP THREE: THE FINANCIAL STATEMENTS

Once the financial data has been recorded, organized into the proper accounts, and added up, we are ready to produce a set of financial statements. In a real business more adjustments, a trial balance, and some other things would have to be done first, but our simplified example still captures the essence of what goes on during the accounting cycle. Let's start by taking a look at a balance sheet constructed from the ledger accounts. If you look back at the ledger accounts you'll see that we've merely transferred the totals we had already calculated to a new format that organizes them in a way that makes it easy to follow this "picture" of the assets, liabilities, and equity we have on a particular date. It's simpler, too, because we don't have to worry about showing debits and credits.

THE BALANCE SHEET:

ASSETS

Cash	$	36,000
Inventory		2,000
Ovens		30,000
Building		55,000
Accumulated Depreciation		(2,000)
Total Assets	$	92,000

LIABILITIES

Accounts Payable	$	3,000
Long-term Debt		35,000
Total Liabilities	$	38,000

OWNER'S EQUITY

Owner's Capital	$	60,000
Retained Earnings		23,000
Total Owner's Equity	$	83,000

Next, there's the income statement. The purpose here is to list all our revenues, all our expenses, and the net income, which is the difference between the two. These numbers are simply taken from where we originally organized them in retained earnings. As with the balance sheet, we're really not saying anything we didn't already know, just putting it in a clear, concise format. If our income is positive it means we made a profit because we were able to get more in return than we had to give up in the process of exchange.

If our income is negative it means we suffered a loss by giving away more than we received in return. As you can see, profits enhance our wealth and cause us to become better off—at least in financial terms. Losses, of course, do the opposite.

INCOME STATEMENT:

REVENUE:
    Sales $ 100,000

EXPENSES:

Cost of Goods Sold	$ 12,000	
Rent	15,000	
Salaries	45,000	
Depreciation	2,000	
Interest	1,000	
Taxes	2,000	
Total Expenses		77,000
NET INCOME		$ 23,000

It looks like we didn't do too bad for our first year in a business known to be highly competitive. By keeping track of our economic activity with an accounting system, after compiling the information, we can look back and analyze how we did. Whatever insight we gain from doing this can then be used to help us plan for the future with the goal of using our limited resources in the most efficient ways possible so that our wealth may be maximized.

Most new businesses invest their profits right back in the business, should they be fortunate enough to have any. In a corporation where there are numerous owners (through stock shares) instead of just one as in this example, some of the profits may be paid out to the owners in the form of dividends. You can see from this example why many younger businesses that are growing don't pay out dividends—they keep the earnings to finance future growth. The owners (stockholders) usually won't mind, so long as they feel that the future growth will make their shares more valuable.

FINANCIAL AND MANAGERIAL ACCOUNTING

Accounting can be separated into two branches, financial and managerial. Financial accounting is concerned with the kinds of things we just saw, such as the recording of financial information and the production of financial statements to be used by managers, creditors, regulators, owners, and other parties to evaluate and make decisions about a business's performance. Financial accounting is guided by a fairly strict set of standards so that users of the information can have a fair degree of certainty that it is reliable and relevant.

The other branch is managerial accounting. It is also concerned with the same economic activity as financial accounting, but for different purposes. In managerial accounting the information is tailored for use by managers in order to guide them in making decisions about how the business should be run. Because managerial accounting isn't geared toward meeting the needs of people outside those who are responsible for operating it, there is much more flexibility in how information is prepared than in financial accounting. A managerial accountant might prepare cash budgets, operating forecasts, analysis of past performance, and the development of strategies, using the same information, but in different formats. Managerial accounting is, in essence, the practical application of the basic theory of microeconomics, which is the subject of the rest of this book.

SUMMARY

- ✓ Accounting is a rational, straightforward system for gathering, organizing, presenting, and evaluating financial information.

- ✓ Accounting operates according to a set of simple concepts that are easily understood.

- ✓ Accounting gets the reputation for being complicated because it is applied to a wide variety of settings where the reality about which accountants are trying to collect data isn't always very clear.

- ✓ Money is used as a common standard for measuring economic activity; it functions as part of the language for communicating information in an accounting system.

- ✓ Only that which can be quantified in dollars and cents is used in an accounting system, not because accountants feel that only money is important, rather, this limitation serves to keep the focus on information that is reliable, verifiable, and stated in units where the value is commonly understood.

- ✓ Accounting is geared toward recording economic activity that consists of exchanges between parties; economic activity is the result of human behavior.

- ✓ An accounting system tells us what we own (assets), what we owe (liabilities), and what is left for the owners after the debts are paid (equity).

✓ Through the use of revenues and expenses, accounting keeps track of the inflow of resources, resources sacrificed for these, and the difference between the two, resulting either in an increase or decrease of wealth.

✓ Our accounting system lets us see how well we are utilizing our limited resources.

✓ In a free market economy it is vital that the participants have access to financial information that has been compiled according to a solid set of standards and is reliable in decision-making.

NEW VOCABULARY

information system
expenses
revenues
profit
loss
assets
depreciation
liabilities
equity
dividends
accounting equation
journal entry
ledgers
balance sheet
income statement
cash flows
owner's equity
financial accounting
managerial accounting

QUESTIONS FOR REVIEW

1. What is accounting, and why are accounting systems necessary?
2. What should a good accounting system do for us?
3. How does the information produced through the use of accounting help us evaluate how well we are utilizing our limited resources?
4. What do opportunity costs have to do with how well, or how poorly, our accounting system says we are doing?

5. What are assets, liabilities, and equity?

6. What are expenses and revenues? Why is the difference between them significant?

7. What are debits and credits? Describe how they affect assets, liabilities, and equity.

8. Discuss the reasons why the accounting equation should always be in balance.

9. What is the purpose of the general journal? Of ledgers?

10. Name the different financial statements discussed and explain what they tell us.

Chapter 4

THE BASICS OF SUPPLY AND DEMAND

LEARNING OBJECTIVES

In this chapter we learn about:

- ✓ How the market system determines prices in the product market—the market for goods and services.
- ✓ How the market mechanism determines prices in the factor market—the market for resources such as land, labor, capital, and entrepreneurship.
- ✓ The reason demand curves generally slope downward.
- ✓ The reason supply curves generally slope upward.
- ✓ How the laws of supply and demand interact to establish market equilibrium prices.
- ✓ The difference between changes in demand and supply and changes in quantity demanded and quantity supplied.
- ✓ How many different factors can cause demand and supply curves to shift.

INTRODUCTION

When you walk into a supermarket you are faced with the interesting problem of choosing what you are going to buy from among 50,000 to 100,000 different items on the shelves. Each item has a price. This brings up a couple of interesting questions. How was that price established? Who made the pricing decision? Furthermore, why are some things so expensive—like lobster or steaks—while others—like salt or flour—are so cheap? Finally, think about why those products are there in the first place. Who made the decision that brought those products to the market shelf? We shall see.

The objective of this chapter is to examine the basic principles of economic theory that explain the operation of the market mechanism. The market mechanism is the process that channels available resources into the production of the goods and services that people want. Markets are usually associated with capitalism which, in turn, is based on institutions such as private ownership of property, freedom to purchase and sell whatever one wishes, and the right to earn profit.

THE CIRCULAR FLOW OF INCOME

The conventional analysis of the free market system is shown in the model Figure 4-1. It demonstrates (very simply) how an economy with an extensive division of labor solves the problems of What, How, and For Whom to produce, which we first ran into in Chapter 1. The market decides. Notice that two types of markets are represented in the figure. In the **product market**, businesses sell their output to households. In the **factor market**, businesses buy inputs from households that they combine to produce goods and services for the product market. These factor inputs (or resources) are traditionally classified as land (including natural resources), labor, capital, and entrepreneurship—which we have defined as a combination of managerial skills, technology, and know-how.

Key Concept: A product market is a market in which a particular good or service is bought and sold.

Key Concept: A factor market is a market in which firms demand natural resources, labor, capital, and know-how from the individuals and households who own them. Factor resources are used to produce goods and services.

Households play two roles in the free market system. All members of households are consumers in the sense that they purchase the goods and services produced by business firms. That's easy enough to understand. But households play another equally important role. In the final analysis households own or supply the factor resources that businesses combine to produce products. It is households that provide the land (space and natural resources), labor, capital (money), and managerial skills in order to produce, distribute, and sell their products. Businesses must pay for these input factors. These payments are made in the form of rent for land, wages for labor, interest for capital, and profits paid to those who are owners of business firms.

In both the product and factor markets the forces of supply and demand determine the prices that are paid for products and the prices that are paid for factor resources. Prices act as signals to all members of the economy. In the same way that traffic lights tell drivers when to stop, go, or prepare to stop, prices tell us how scarce the product or factor is that we may wish to buy. For example, if the price of wheat goes up we can surmise that there is relatively less wheat in the market than before the price change. Such a change in price could be due to an increase in demand or a decrease in supply, or both. Whatever the reason, the higher price signals to the consumer that due to the greater relative scarcity of wheat, it will take more money to get X amount of wheat or Y amount of bread. This, in turn, implies that a consumer will have to give up something else (like some butter or beans) to continue consuming the same amount of wheat. Prices are thus, in theory, viewed as signals indicating relative scarcity.

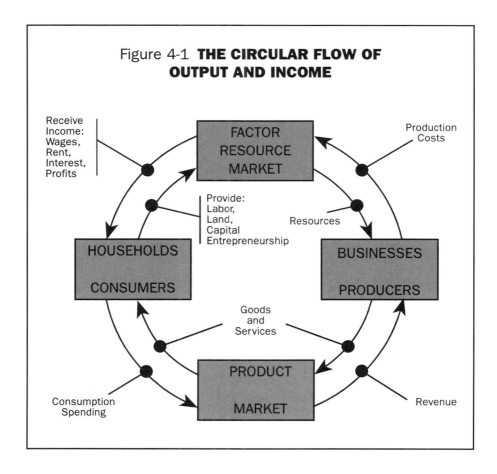

Figure 4-1 **THE CIRCULAR FLOW OF OUTPUT AND INCOME**

Given that consumers' range of desires for goods and services is almost always greater than their ability to purchase them, lower prices allow consumers to acquire a greater amount of goods and increase their total satisfaction. However, sellers usually find that they can improve their financial position by charging higher prices for their goods. Consequently, buyers and sellers (who are, interestingly, the same people playing different roles) have different interests. As buyers, they want to buy at a low price, while as sellers they want to sell at a high price. These opposing goals are moderated in the marketplace by the laws of supply and demand.

SUPPLY AND DEMAND: THE BASICS

Since the concept of supply and demand is so important and basic to almost all of economic theory, it merits special attention. The words "supply" and "demand" are, of course, part of our everyday vocabulary, so it is easy for people to think they understand these concepts—and miss the essence of how the free market system really works. Let's begin by taking the simplest possible example.

The Demand Curve

We have said that consumers will usually buy more of any given item if the price is reduced. But the question is: How much more? Business people need to know how consumers will react to increases or decreases in prices. They can find out by studying market research data on consumer behavior, or they can experiment with a controlled group of consumers to see how they in fact react to price changes. Then, armed with this data, they can begin to verify the hypothesis that more of a given item will be bought at lower prices. For convenience, then, the data can be presented either in a schedule or on a graph.

Let's assume that we have studied the market demand for wheat, and that our conclusions are embodied in Figure 4-2. There we see that if wheat has a price of $6 a bushel, consumers will want to buy 20 million bushels. As the price is lowered they will want to buy more. If the price falls to $2 they will purchase 60 million bushels. We have now established a demand curve for wheat, which illustrates a tentative hypothesis about how consumers will behave with respect to price changes for this particular commodity. As we shall see, this hypothesis has a number of real world uses.

In summary, we have described here in simplified form the **Law of Demand**, which states that: *as prices are reduced more can be sold*, or put differently, *consumers will buy more at lower prices*. This means that consumer demand is a function of price, that is, $D = f(P)$. In that context it is

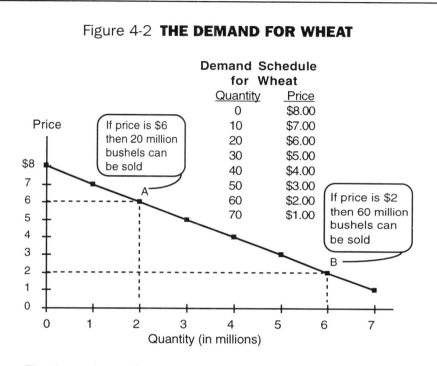

Figure 4-2 **THE DEMAND FOR WHEAT**

The demand curve for wheat is derived from the demand schedule for wheat. Price is on the vertical axis and quantity on the horizontal axis. At point A the price is $6 per bushel and the quantity demanded is 20 million bushels. At point B, price is $2 per bushel and quantity demanded is 60 million bushels. This illustrates the law of demand, which states that there is an inverse relationship between price and quantity demanded. As price increases, *ceteris paribus*, quantity demanded will decrease and as price decreases the quantity demanded will increase.

important to recognize that price and quantity demanded are inversely related. When price goes down, quantity demanded increases, and when price goes up, demand will go down.

 Key Concept: The Law of Demand is the general observation that as prices are lowered for a given product consumers will want to purchase more of it.

The Supply Curve

The corresponding question, of course, is: How much are producers willing to supply? We can begin to answer it by studying the behavior of suppliers, or producers. It should come as no surprise that producer are always willing to produce/supply more of any product if they can sell it for a higher price. However, because resources are limited (scarce) as more of them are used in the production process they become more expensive. Consequently, producers in most cases will produce more only if there is a real possibility that they can sell the product at a higher price. Engineers and cost accountants are hired to analyze the physical production possibilities of a firm and determine exactly how much more it will cost to increase production by a specific quantity. With that data, a supply schedule and a supply curve can be constructed that, as Figure 4-3 shows, will generally slope upward.

The supply curve for wheat is derived from the supply schedule for wheat, which records a series of prices and the corresponding quantity that can be sold at each price. On the graph, at a price of $2 per bushel the quantity supplied is 20 million bushels. At a price of $6 per bushel the quantity supplied is 60 million bushels. The curve illustrates the law of supply, which states the relationship between price and quantity for suppliers. As price increases the quantity supplied will increase, and as price decreases the quantity supplied will also decrease.

This, then, in simple form, is the rationale behind the **Law of Supply**, which states that: *producers will supply more of any given product when the price is increased.* Therefore, supply (like demand) is also a function of price, that is, $S = f(P)$. In a supply context price, and quantity supplied are directly related. As price increases, producers will be willing to produce more; as price goes down they will want to produce less.

 Key Concept: The Law of Supply states that as the price of any given product is increased producers will want to supply more of it.

Equilibrium

Now let's combine these two opposing concepts—the theory that demand curves slope downward while supply curves slope upward—on one graph, as we have done in Figure 4-4. Doing this shows us how the market forces of free competition will sooner or later arrive at a point where the demand curve crosses the supply curve. This point indicates the price and quantity that will satisfy both consumers and producers and optimize the best interests of each.

Remember that supply and demand are determined by different factors. Actors in the market are simply acting in their own self-interest, buyers trying to economize and buy as cheaply as possible, while producers are trying to maximize their incomes by selling for as high as possible. In a free market, the competition between the buyers and sellers (and, the competition among the members of each group) eventually determines the actual market price at which the product will be sold—the prevailing market price. This is commonly called the equilibrium price.

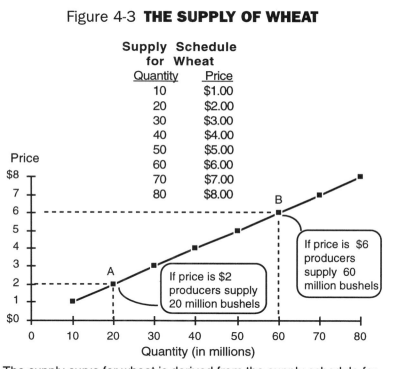

Figure 4-3 **THE SUPPLY OF WHEAT**

Supply Schedule for Wheat

Quantity	Price
10	$1.00
20	$2.00
30	$3.00
40	$4.00
50	$5.00
60	$6.00
70	$7.00
80	$8.00

If price is $2 producers supply 20 million bushels

If price is $6 producers supply 60 million bushels

The supply curve for wheat is derived from the supply schedule for wheat. With price on the vertical axis and quantity on the horizontal axis, at point A the price is $2 per bushel and the quantity supplied is 20 million bushels. At point B, price is $6 per bushel and quantity supplied is 60 million bushels. This illustrates the law of supply, which states that there is a direct relationship between price and quantity supplied. As price increases, *ceteris paribus*, quantity supplied will increase and as the price decreases the quantity supplied will decrease.

DEMAND AND SUPPLY AT EQUILIBRIUM

As we have seen in Figures 4-2 and 4-3, the demand and supply curves for wheat indicate that consumers will buy more wheat at lower prices and producers will supply more wheat at higher prices. The interplay of the forces of demand and supply will bring about a price and quantity that will reflect the interests of both the consumer and producer. Figure 4-4 illustrates how the market mechanism works, which in this case leads to an equilibrium price of $4 per bushel and an output level of 40 million bushels.

The dynamics of the market mechanism can be understood by analyzing the relationship between price and quantity from either a surplus or shortage perspective. At a price of $6 per bushel suppliers are willing to produce 60 million bushels, but consumers are only willing (or able) to buy 20 million, so a *surplus* exists. On the other hand, at a price of $2 consumers demand 60 million but suppliers are willing to produce only 20 million bushels, so there is a shortage.

A surplus sets in action market forces (because of competition) between sellers, which causes them to lower prices and eliminate the surplus. A shortage causes consumers to compete with each other and bid up the price.

Where and when will this all end? It will end when the forces of supply and demand have balanced at an **equilibrium** point, which on our graph is where the two curves intersect at point E. At that point the prevailing market price will be $4; the amount produced and consumed will be 40 million bushels. How long will that price last? It will prevail until some outside disturbance comes along to change producers' willingness to sell wheat or consumers' willingness to buy it. *Ceteris paribus*, the $4 price would prevail forever until "everything else is not equal," that is, until some external factor comes along to change the situation.

Key Concept: Equilibrium in a market is the point where there are neither shortages nor surpluses.

SHIFTS IN DEMAND CURVES

In the real world, except under experimental conditions, everything is not usually equal. Consequently, while the notion that demand is a function of price has a certain amount of theoretical elegance, it doesn't explain the determination of prices very well. The reason is there are many other factors besides price that affect consumer and producer behavior. We have shown that under certain strictly specified conditions, a change in price will bring about a change in the quantity demanded or the quantity supplied. That is, the price change will cause a movement up or down the demand curve depending on whether the price was increased or decreased. But what if there is a change in everybody's desire to purchase this product? Then we face a different situation.

Figure 4-4 **THE SUPPLY AND DEMAND OF WHEAT**

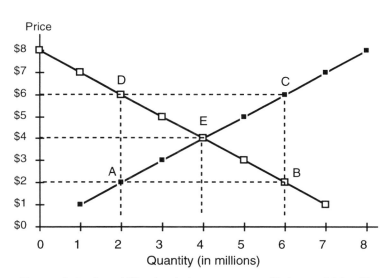

At a market price of $6 a bushel, consumers will demand 20 million bushels (point D) while producers are actually willing to supply 60 million (point C). Therefore, at a price of $6 a surplus (of 40 million bushels) will exist. Whenever there is a surplus in the market, competition between sellers will force the price downward.

At a market price of $2, producers will only be willing to supply 20 million bushels (point A) while consumers will demand 60 million bushels (point B). Therefore, at a price of $2 a shorage will exist. Whenever there is a shortage, competition between buyers will force the price upward.

Eventually, these two opposing forces will cause the market price to settle at the intersection of the supply and demand curves (point E).

REASONS FOR SHIFTS IN DEMAND

There are a number of reasons why demand curves shift. Among them are changes in tastes, changes in the price of relative goods—such as complementary or substitutable products—and changes in incomes. Let's consider each in more detail.

Tastes

Let's suppose, for example, that a new health fad comes along—as it did in the late 1980s—and people begin substituting oats for wheat. That will mean the demand curve for wheat (at any price) will shift to the left, while the demand curve for oats will shift to the right. So, a change in consumers' tastes will shift the entire demand schedule rather than simply move the equilibrium price to a higher or lower level. There are many other examples. The development of cassette tapes and, later, compact discs caused a dramatic shift in the demand for old-fashioned long-play albums, which have all but disappeared. Tastes for different kinds of music, which are notoriously fickle, shift demand curves for one kind of music every few years. Changes in smoking habits in recent years have caused a downward shift in the demand for cigarettes, and so on.

Now, in the past few pages we have discussed two different concepts that can sometimes be confused. It is important to distinguish between changes in quantity demanded and changes in overall demand. What do these terms mean? The first, a change in quantity demanded, is caused by price changes. This kind of change is represented by *movement up or down* along the demand curve. A change in overall demand, on the other hand, is caused by changes in non-price factors, such as tastes. It results in *a shift in the entire demand curve*. Therefore, it is important to remember that changes in quantity demanded and changes in demand are not the same thing.

Complements and Substitutes

In addition to changes in consumer taste, many other factors external to the basic price-quantity relationship, such as changes in the price of related products, can shift supply and demand curves. To say the least, they play havoc with business production plans. For example, a large range of common products have complementary relationships to other products. Coffee sales are partly dependent on the price of cream and sugar. A disturbance in the sugar market that causes sugar prices to rise will cause a decrease in the demand for coffee. That is, it will shift the demand curve for coffee down and to the left. Large increases in coffee prices, as have occurred several times in the past decade, will correspondingly affect the demand for cream and sugar. There are many other examples of **complementary products**: beer and pretzels, automobiles and tires and gasoline, bagels and lox, and so on. Such products are related inversely in the sense that a decrease in the price of one causes an increase in demand for the other.

Key Concept: Complementary products are those in which a change in price of one will cause the demand for both to move in the opposite direction. That is, there is an inverse relationship between price and quantity demanded.

Also, changes in the price of **substitutable goods**, which are relatively common, will cause demand curves to shift. For example, coffee and tea are, to a certain extent, substitutes for each other in the sense that they both do the same job. A decrease in the price of one will shift the demand curve for the other as consumers shift their expenditures to the lower-priced product. That is, there is a direct relationship between price and quantity demanded.

Key Concept: Substitutable goods are those in which a change in the price of one will cause the demand for the other to move in the same direction. That is, there is a direct relationship between price and quantity.

Changes in Income

Obviously, when consumers' incomes change their pattern of demand for different products also changes. There is, however, a subtle difference in the way that income increases affect demand. Typically, when your income increases you will tend to buy more of everything, but not always. With a higher level of income you might buy more airline tickets, or filet mignon, or more CDs, or expensive clothes. Such products are called "normal goods" in the sense that it is normal to buy more of them as your income increases.

But some products are not normal in respect to income changes, with a higher income you will most likely buy less of some products. For example, chances are you would not buy cheap hamburger, cassette tapes, and cheap clothes. Such products are called "inferior goods" in the sense that fewer of them will be bought as incomes increase. The difference between normal and inferior goods is a subtle but important one, especially if you are a business person trying to decide how consumers will respond to your product in a climate of rising or falling incomes.

Shifts in Supply Curves

Supply curves, like demand curves, also are subject to external forces that can shift them upward or downward. However, the reasons are different. Most commonly, supply conditions are affected by improvements in production techniques, and new technology that permit more to be produced at the same or lower price. New developments such as robots, computers, and other automated production techniques have dramatically lowered the price of many products in recent years, especially in the consumer electronics industry. The improvements make firms more productive and shift supply curves to the right (downward) because more can be produced for a lower price at any level of production.

On the other hand, disturbances in markets for resources used in the production process can shift supply curves upward. A drought in the midwestern agricultural states will cause increases in food prices. A sudden increase in oil prices, such as happened in the 1970s and early 1990s, will raise production costs for almost all industries, shifting the supply curve upward to the left. Conversely, a drop in resource input prices will shift the supply curve downward to the right.

The important question now becomes: Why do supply and demand curves shift? It merits careful study. Later, we shall see that there are even more factors involved in explaining the behavior of consumers and business firms as each goes about the business of acting rationally in their own self-interest. And we will see how supply and demand analysis can be used to explain a number of other issues such as the effects of governmentally imposed price controls, the effects of the minimum wage laws, tariffs, and controls on foreign exchange.

SUMMARY

- ✓ In a capitalist economy the market mechanism determines the allocation of scarce resources.
- ✓ The free play of the forces of supply and demand determines the price and output level for goods and services
- ✓ A change in the *quantity demanded* or supplied is a result of a change in the price of the good, which results in a movement along the demand or supply curve.
- ✓ The basic determinants of *demand* are tastes and preferences, the price complements and substitutes, incomes, and the price of the good.
- ✓ The basic determinants of supply are technology, price of factor inputs, and the price of the good.

NEW VOCABULARY

factor market	equilibrium
product market	complementary products
law of demand	substitutable goods
law of supply	

QUESTIONS FOR REVIEW

1. How does the circular flow of income illustrate the market mechanism?
2. What is the difference between the factor (resource) market and the product market?
3. What is the basic Law of Demand? Law of Supply?
4. What is a substitute good?
5. What is a complementary good?
6. What are the basic determinants of demand? Supply?
7. What is the difference between a change in demand and a change in quantity demanded?
8. What is the difference between a change in supply and a change in quantity supplied?
9. What is meant by the term equilibrium?
10. What might cause a shift in a demand curve?

Chapter 5

BEHIND THE DEMAND CURVE

LEARNING OBJECTIVES

In this chapter we will learn more about:

- ✓ How utility analysis explains consumer behavior.
- ✓ How the relationship between the extra satisfaction obtained from a purchase and its price determines the shape of demand curves.
- ✓ How the market system gives us all a bonus we didn't ask for.
- ✓ How consumers make rational choices about what they purchase.
- ✓ Why demand curves slope downward.
- ✓ How changes in other variables besides price affect demand curves.

INTRODUCTION

When you walk into a large supermarket you are faced with shelves and bins filled with as many as 100,000 different items. How do you choose among them, especially if your grocery budget is limited? How do you decide what to buy? In this chapter our overall objective is to learn more about consumer behavior, and especially how consumers make rational choices among many alternatives. We learn how consumer behavior is affected by budget constraints in the context of wants as compared to needs. The chapter also introduces us to some basic tools of economics that are useful not only in economic analysis generally but are especially useful to marketing researchers and advertisers, who are constantly trying to figure out ways to increase sales. Their job is easier if they know how and why consumers choose to buy certain products. Buyers can also use these tools. If you understand the rationality of consumer decision-making, you may be less likely to be persuaded to make irrational choices.

On another level, this chapter will sharpen our understanding of demand curves, how they are constructed, why they slope as they do, and why they are useful to business firms in marketing their products.

THE THEORY OF CONSUMER DEMAND

First of all, we need to recall from our earlier discussion that a capitalist economy is presumed to be driven by consumer sovereignty—the notion that "the consumer is king." The decisions that businesses make about what to produce and sell are based on their assessment of consumers' desires and willingness to express those desires in the marketplace with dollar votes.

Needs Versus Wants

You may be yearning for a cashmere sweater, but how badly do you need it? Would an old sweater from a thrift store keep you just as warm? Economists, like other people, distinguish between **consumer needs** and consumer wants. And they also study how people develop a set of wants. Basic needs such as food, clothing, and shelter are relatively simple to identify and are regarded as a portion of every consumer's wants. Wants and desires cover more territory. Consumer behavior theory generally assumes that wants are unlimited, which is another way of saying no matter how much money we have, we always find a way of disposing of it—a notion that most of us have probably experienced at one level or another, and one that keeps jewelers in business.

 Key Concept: Consumer needs include food, shelter, and clothing. Wants are determined by cultural conditioning.

The idea of unlimited wants also suggests that each person brings a private set of preferences to the market along with a certain ability to pay. That set of wants is assumed by some economists (and psychologists) to be a natural and intuitive part of consumer behavior. Others, however, argue that wants above needs are determined by one's social class, educational level, peer group, and so on, and often lead to irrational consumer purchasing decisions. This, they say, tends to divert productive activities toward some consumers' unnecessary wants and away from others' needs.

Still others argue that many consumer wants in a capitalist society are determined not by socially induced preferences or intuitive desires but by the pervasiveness of advertising. These critics contend that advertising conditions us to think we want (and thus need) certain products, when the reality is that producers need to sell them more than consumers need to have them. Most television commercials seem to support the argument.

These complications duly noted, it will simplify matters here to assume that wants in general are unlimited (everybody wants more then they have) and that the summation of all consumers' wants, coupled with their ability to pay, determines what will be produced in a free market economy. Further, we shall assume for now that consumers make *rational decisions* about what they need and want. These assumptions approximate most people's real-life situations closely enough to allow for a reasonably useful analysis of the theory of consumer behavior.

Wants and Demand

It is important to recognize that wants, which tend to be unlimited and unruly, are not the same thing as demand. That is, *a demand curve is not a "want curve."* A demand curve relates a given quantity to a given price, the price that consumers are estimated to be willing and able to pay. Demanding something to the extent that you are willing to go to the marketplace and buy it is quite different from simply wanting something but not having the money to buy it. It hardly needs to be pointed out that most of us want many things beyond what our income allows us to purchase.

Satisfaction and Utility

As this discussion proceeds we will often use the somewhat technical term **utility** to connote the amount of satisfaction one obtains from purchasing and consuming a product. The term entered the lexicon of economics in the 1870s when economists first tried to analyze consumer behavior in terms of the amount of satisfaction a person got from the purchase of a product or service. Their attempt to quantify utility forms the basis of modern consumer theory.

 Key Concept: Utility is the amount of satisfaction one gets from consuming or having a product.

Measurement Problems

The level of satisfaction you attain from purchasing and consuming a product may vary considerably from the satisfaction that others get from it. That is simply another way of saying that people have different tastes. Your tastes in music are—we would wager—quite different from those of your parents. Consequently, if we want to measure the satisfaction you get out of having the latest rock music CD, we would need a different scale to measure it. After all, your parents would probably have a different level of satisfaction (or dissatisfaction) from owning the same disc. Indeed, everybody has different patterns of utility because everybody has different tastes. If they didn't, life would be pretty boring.

Moreover, some argue that since levels of satisfaction are a personal, internal phenomenon, it may not be possible to measure utility at all. How many units of satisfaction do you get out of consuming a soft drink? You can't answer that question because there is no standard unit of measurement to quantify utility. But it *is possible* to assign numbers arbitrarily to different levels of satisfaction, even though the numbers will vary with different individuals and different products. Such arbitrary assignment of units of satisfaction—called "utils" of utility—allows us to extrapolate the sum of a large group of consumers' utility "schedules" into a generalization about consumer behavior, which we call a demand curve. All that is necessary is to recognize a quantifiable behavioral relationship between levels of satisfaction gained from consuming a product and the price that must be paid for it. We will see how to do this later in the chapter.

Diminishing Marginal Utility

One further clarification will allow us to proceed. The one aspect of consumer satisfaction common to all consumers is that each *additional unit* of any product consumed in a given time period is likely to yield a declining amount of satisfaction. How much satisfaction do you get from consuming one Pepsi™? We don't know, but we do know that in any given day the amount of satisfaction you get from drinking a Pepsi™ will decline as you drink additional units of it. That's easy to understand if you just think about the satisfaction you get from the first Pepsi™ of the day and compare it to how you would feel after the seventeenth Pepsi™ you consumed in the same day. It's even easier to understand if you to try to visualize how many BMWs you might buy if you won the lottery. One would probably give you a lot of satisfaction, two might be nice for a change of pace, but three would begin to crowd your driveway. And five would be a real nuisance—your front yard would look like a used car lot!

The point of this seemingly frivolous diversion is that consumption of succeeding units of almost everything is subject to declining levels of additional satisfaction. In economics this is called the **principle of diminishing marginal utility**. Notice that it is called a principle rather than an assumption. This is because the hypothesis has been tested and re-tested thousands of times and because it also conforms to everyone's perception of reality. You can test it yourself by trying to think of exceptions. Is there anything that doesn't leave you with less satisfaction the more you have of it? The only one we can think of is education: the more you have of it, the more you want—we hope.

 Key Concept: The principle of diminishing marginal utility is the idea that consuming additional units of anything in a given time period will give you successively less additional satisfaction.

The Assumptions of Utility Theory

In the next section we will see how all this can be useful in analyzing consumer behavior in particular and consumer demand in general. But before we proceed it may be useful to summarize the basic principles we have examined so far and, especially, the assumptions behind them.

1. Wants are assumed to be unlimited for consumers in general but limited when we are considering only one consumer's desire for one product.
2. Incomes are limited (for most people), so everyone has to make rational choices among different possible purchases within the constraint of a given budget.
3. The sum of our desires is almost always greater than our income.
4. Because people have different tastes, it is the satisfaction one gets out of a particular purchase that counts, not the product itself.
5. Consumer decisions are rational, in the sense that a person tries to balance the utility received from a purchase against the disutility (opportunity cost) of giving up the money that could have been used to buy something else.
6. The principle of diminishing marginal utility applies to the consumption of any product. The first unit will usually give you more satisfaction than additional units.[1]

TOTAL AND MARGINAL UTILITY

Do you like to eat popcorn? How much popcorn? Can you even get enough popcorn? The difference between the total utility (satisfaction) we get out of consuming several units of a product and the marginal (extra) satisfaction we get out of consuming an additional unit of it is an important distinction.

---

[1] There may be a few exceptions to this assumption. In a large family the second color TV may yield more satisfaction than the first because it eliminates the battles over what to watch. A second car may have a similar effect. But, eventually, as more units are purchased, diminishing utility sets in.

Figure 5-1a shows the total utility gained from eating popcorn over, say, a four-hour period at a double-feature movie. **Total utility** is the sum of satisfaction achieved as additional units are consumed. **Marginal utility** (Figure 5-1b) is the additional satisfaction from consuming each additional unit. The assignment of units of utility—"utils"—is arbitrary and would vary among individuals, depending on how hungry they were on that particular evening and their taste for popcorn.

 Key Concept: Total utility is the sum of the satisfaction gained by consuming a given number of units of a product.

 Key Concept: Marginal utility is the amount of satisfaction gained by consuming one additional unit of a product.

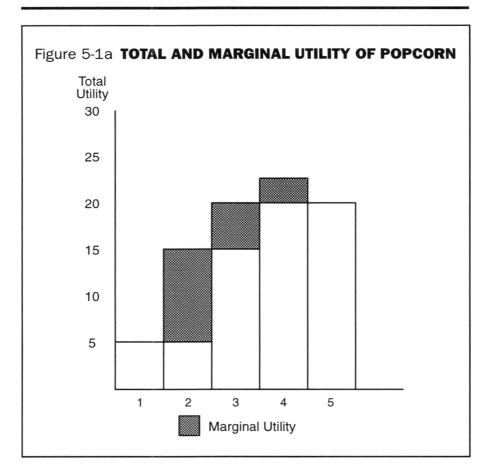

Figure 5-1a **TOTAL AND MARGINAL UTILITY OF POPCORN**

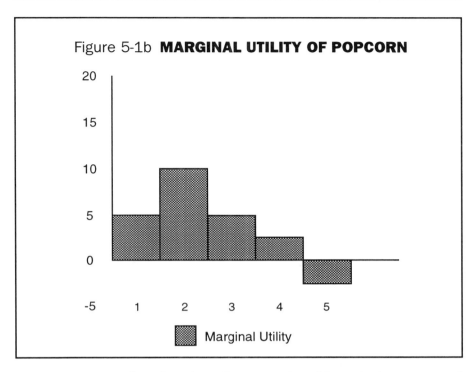

Figure 5-1b **MARGINAL UTILITY OF POPCORN**

The consumption of one bag of popcorn gives this particular consumer 5 utils of satisfaction, and the second bag (our experiments indicate) provides more satisfaction than the first, say 10 utils. Look again at Figure 5-1a. The total utility derived from the consumption of two bags is 15 utils. At the same time, we can see in Figure 5-1b that the marginal utility derived from the second bag is 10 utils. The total is simply the sum of the marginal utils.

This concept—total versus marginal—deserves careful study since it is basic to much of economic theory. In fact, it forms the basis of both the theory of demand and the theory of supply. In terms of our popcorn story, the question is: Do we stop eating popcorn when *total* utility starts to decline, or when *marginal* utility starts to decline?

As we continue to eat popcorn, we can well believe that the marginal utility derived from it will decrease, as the graphs clearly indicate. After the seventh bag of popcorn the marginal utility (or satisfaction) is, in fact, likely to become negative (somewhere around the time you are beginning to feel sick). At this point the rational consumer would stop eating popcorn and turn to some other activity that would give more satisfaction, such as taking an Alka Seltzer™.

This example illustrates the distinction we made earlier. Although wants in general are assumed to be unlimited, the desire for any particular good diminishes as more of it is consumed.

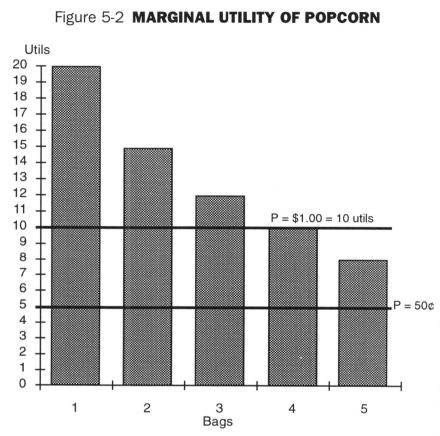

Figure 5-2 **MARGINAL UTILITY OF POPCORN**

How much popcorn would you buy? The market price for one bag of popcorn is $1.00 or 10 utils. A consumer would continue to buy additional bags of popcorn until the satisfaction of the last unit purchased exactly equals the market price. In this example, at a market price of $1.00, the consumer would stop consumption after buying 4 bags of popcorn because the 5th bag of popcorn would yield only 8 utils of satisfaction, which is less than the market price.

What does all this tell us about consumer behavior? Nothing much except that it doesn't take long for one's desire to become saturated by any particular product if enough of it is made available. However, if we add one more variable to this simple model we have, in essence, demonstrated the basic theory behind the demand curve. That variable is price.

Assume that popcorn sells for $1 per bag, and that the utility of money to you is ten utils per dollar, or 10 cents each.[2] How many bags of popcorn would you buy? This situation is shown in Figure 5-2. Since the first bag of popcorn gives you 20 utils of satisfaction and you only have to give up ten utils (at 10 cents each) you would clearly want to buy it. And, since you know that the second bag is going to give you 15 units of satisfaction and will still cost only 10 utils, you would buy that bag and continue to buy more until the point that the satisfaction from your next purchase is barely equal to the utility value of the money you would have to give up. In this example your purchase of popcorn would logically stop after 4 bags because the 5th bag would give you only 8 utils of satisfaction, compared to the 10 utils you have to give up to buy it. The important comparison here is between the satisfaction you get from consuming an additional unit of the product and the loss of satisfaction you experience from giving up the money to buy it, especially considering that you could spend the money on something else.

This example illustrates an important point: Total and marginal utility schedules suggest that one would rationally stop consuming goods at the point where their total utility becomes negative. We can see, however, that since all goods have a price, the relevant comparison is instead between *price and marginal utility*, not total utility. That is, rational consumers will purchase more of any product up to the point where price equals marginal utility, or P = MU. In addition, this example provides us with a logical explanation for one of the assumptions we made in previous chapters, which is: *demand curves (almost always) slope downward.*

Look again at Figure 5-2. What would a rational consumer (with this assumed utility preference pattern) do if the price of popcorn were lowered to, say, 50 cents? Buy more popcorn, obviously. In fact, we can assume with some certainty that more of nearly anything can be sold at a lower price, which is all that demand curves presume to illustrate. Also, it should now be clear why we emphasized earlier that the theory of demand depends on the theory of diminishing marginal utility. Lowering the price makes more units of an item come into the range where the diminishing utility of each unit exceeds the disutility of giving up the money to buy it.

The Consumer Surplus

Armed with this basic understanding of classical utility theory we can now understand why most economists argue that the market system works to the benefit of all. As a rational consumer, how much would you pay for the

---

[2]   This is a simplifying assumption, because money may have different utility value for different people, depending on their income or wealth.

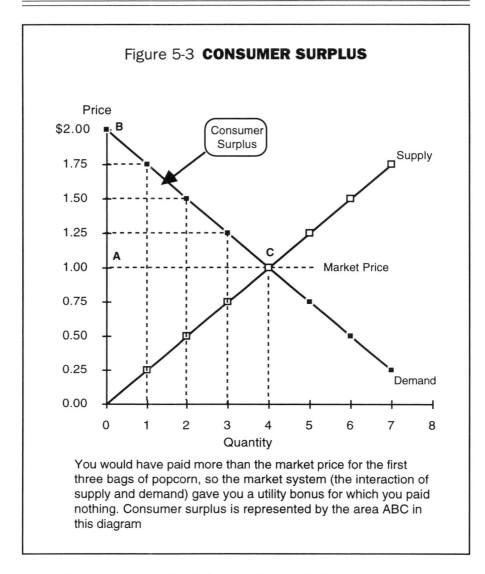

Figure 5-3 **CONSUMER SURPLUS**

You would have paid more than the market price for the first three bags of popcorn, so the market system (the interaction of supply and demand) gave you a utility bonus for which you paid nothing. Consumer surplus is represented by the area ABC in this diagram

second bag of popcorn? Certainly more than the $1 it costs. You would, in fact pay as much as $1.50 for it, the value (at 10 cents per util) of the utility you expect to get from it. But since you pay only the *market price*, the price set in the marketplace by the laws of supply and demand, you actually receive utility bonus of (in this case) 5 utils. (What bonus do you receive from the third purchase?)

Because the market charges the same price to everyone, you normally earn a **consumer surplus** on most purchases if you live in a market economy.

This concept, which was developed by English economist Alfred Marshall around 1890, is illustrated in Figure 5-3, which shows that if the market price were $1 and a consumer would have paid $2 for the first unit consumed, $1.50 for the second, $1.25 for the third, they reap a utility bonus—a consumer surplus—for the first three units purchased at the market price. Therefore, the consumer surplus is the area below the demand curve that is above the market price, or triangle A B C.

 Key Concept: The consumer surplus is the bonus you get from paying the market price instead of a price equal to your own money-utility equation.

The Rational Consumer

Our popcorn aficionado faces choices about only one good, which is a quite simplified model of the real world. Even a consumer with a very low income is faced with choices among a large number of different products, all of which have at least some utility.

Suppose, as shown in Figure 5-4, you are trying to decide how to allocate your limited budget among three different products—popcorn, magazines, and kumquats—and your utility schedule for each is different. You prefer popcorn to magazines and magazines to kumquats. Given a market price for each, what will you buy? Clearly you will buy some popcorn first, then a magazine or two to read while you are eating it. But at the high price of kumquats, you won't buy any of them. Why not? Because, given your utility schedule for kumquats, the

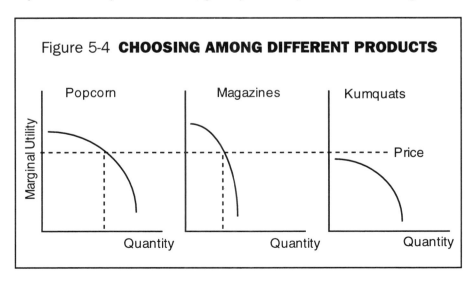

Figure 5-4 **CHOOSING AMONG DIFFERENT PRODUCTS**

disutility of giving up the money will always exceed the utility you would get from spending your money on kumquats, especially with the alternative option of buying popcorn and magazines. (Note, however, that if the price was lowered, kumquats might come into your rational purchase range.)

This rule, like many in economics, merely formalizes common sense. While you don't write down the exact number of utils when deciding whether to buy a new sweater or a new CD of your favorite group, you roughly calculate the pleasure the purchase will give you for the price.

SUMMARY

- ✓ Over the years economists have developed some rather sophisticated ways to describe and predict consumer behavior.

- ✓ One is utility analysis, based on the law of diminishing returns, which posits that consumers make rational choices between possible consumption items on the basis of the utility or satisfaction to be derived from them. This is a basic premise of demand theory.

- ✓ In thinking about consumer behavior it is important to distinguish between consumers' desires and wants as opposed to their needs. Needs, such as food, shelter, and clothing, are quite different from wants, which are often influenced by advertising or other cultural influences.

- ✓ Wants are generally assumed to be unlimited, but budgets are almost always limited. Therefore, demand curves must be viewed in terms of purchasing power.

- ✓ A "want curve" is not a demand curve until wants are backed up by the ability and willingness to buy.

- ✓ The terms "satisfaction" and "utility" mean the same thing. Both are difficult to measure because people have different tastes.

- ✓ The principle of diminishing marginal utility is the backbone of the theory of consumer behavior. It states that satisfaction diminishes after consuming each additional unit of any product.

- ✓ Total utility curves measure the total satisfaction obtained from consuming additional units of a consumer good. Marginal utility curves measure satisfaction at the margin—that is, the utility obtained from each extra unit consumed. The total is always the sum of the marginal.

- ✓ The relevant comparison in determining why demand curves slope downward is between the marginal utility of money and the marginal utility of the product being purchased. Since marginal utility diminishes with the consumption of additional units, sellers must lower price in order to sell more units.

✓ One result of the free market system is that consumers only pay the market price for any product, although because of diminishing utility they would be willing to pay more for the first units they buy. This utility bonus the market gives us is called consumer surplus.

✓ When choosing among two or more goods, rational consumers distribute their purchases in such a way that the marginal utility-price ratios are the same for all the choices available to them. Any other choice is irrational.

NEW VOCABULARY

consumer needs   utility
marginal utility   diminishing marginal utility
total utility   consumer surplus
consumer wants

REVIEW QUESTIONS

1. Suppose consumer demand did not determine what was to be produced. Can you suggest other ways to make these decisions?

2. Why is the distinction between wants and demand so important to demand theory? To business firms?

3. Can you think of any situations where demand curves would not slope downward?

4. Suppose demand for any particular good was not subject to diminishing utility. What then would be the slope of the demand curve? Can you think of any goods that are not subject to diminishing utility?

5. What is meant by the old proverb, "One person's junk is another's treasure"?

Chapter 6

BEHIND THE SUPPLY CURVE

LEARNING OBJECTIVES

The main purpose of this chapter is to analyze the process by which producers make rational decisions about how to combine scarce resources to produce useful products at the least possible economic cost. This process, *the theory of production*, is of extreme importance to any organization that produces anything for sale. The theory of production is a body of thought about the relationship between inputs of the factors of production and output in the context of the economic costs. Specifically, in this chapter we learn about:

✓ how a firm's production output is a function of its inputs.

✓ how the law of diminishing returns affects output at different levels of production.

✓ how costs curves also reflect the law of diminishing returns.

✓ the difference between fixed and variable costs.

✓ why average costs curves are U-shaped.

✓ why the marginal (extra) costs curves play an important role in business decision making.

✓ how these tools can be applied to analyze a small business firm's cost and efficiency profile.

✓ why there is an important difference between the law of diminishing returns in the short run and economies of scale in the long run.

INTRODUCTION

The Production Process

The process of production—the process of combining land, labor, capital, and managerial skills to produce a given product—has certain characteristics that are common to all economies. The technological aspects of production certainly are much the same everywhere. Decisions about *what* to produce and the choice of various combinations of inputs are sometimes made by government and sometimes by business and are different from one economy to another. But these days, in most countries most production decisions are made by businesses.[1]

The production process can be viewed from two distinctly different perspectives. The input view analyzes the behavior of output when factor inputs are increased or decreased. The output view focuses on the behavior of costs as output is increased or decreased. The object of both perspectives is to help business people know how to combine inputs in the most efficient way and to set their output at the level that maximizes production with the least amount of input. In other words, the goal of both the input perspective and the output perspective is to enable the manager to set a production level that maximizes profits.

The physical and financial process of producing almost anything, while it sounds simple, is really rather complicated. The owner or manager of any business has to decide what combination of inputs (land, labor, capital, and entrepreneurship or managerial skill) will provide the maximum output at least cost. Let's look at how this works from the input perspective first.

THE INPUT SIDE

We know from experience that we can increase efficiency if several people are employed to work together, with each one specializing in one stage of the process. In a pizza parlor, for example, one cook can prepare the dough, while another fixes the toppings, another watches the oven, and so on. However, these increases in productivity are lost after a certain point because the oven will only hold so many pizzas and because only so many cooks can work in one small kitchen. Eventually, both productivity and efficiency are lost from having, as the saying goes, "too many cooks in the kitchen." In other words, the business soon encounters the law of diminishing returns.

The Law of Diminishing Returns

The classic case of diminishing returns is the old argument, "You can't grow the world's food supply in a flower pot," which seems silly until you start to analyze it, or until you try growing some patio tomatoes. What is needed to grow tomatoes in a flower pot? You need seeds, soil, water, fertilizer, some sunlight, and a pot. Once you get set up, some of your inputs—the pot, seed, and soil—are fixed in the sense that they can't be varied. The only problem remaining is to decide how much fertilizer, sun, and water are needed. If you want to grow the world's supply of tomatoes on your patio it would

---

[1]   You should recall that we earlier defined microeconomics as the science of allocating scarce resources among alternative ends.

seem to make sense to add as much fertilizer, sun, and water as you could find. But that won't work for reasons with which we are all familiar. Too much of any one thing will kill the plant, so these inputs added to our fixed factors are subject to **the law of diminishing returns**.

 Key Concept: The law of diminishing returns states that when the amount of one input is fixed while others are varied, the marginal product of all inputs will at some point begin to decline.

To generalize from this example, we can say that at the level of a single firm, factor inputs tend to be subject to diminishing returns whenever one factor is varied while the others are held constant. If we assume that the law of diminishing returns holds for all variable resources, it follows that there will be some point in increasing output at which total costs will begin to increase at an increasing rate. If resources have diminishing returns, then more and more resources have to be added to get equivalent increases in output. But to use more resources costs more. When diminishing returns set in, the total costs of production will increase at an increasing rate. In order to produce an extra or additional unit of output it will cost more than the last additional unit of output because more resources will be required. This process is called a "production function" because the production of a given output is a function of the amount of input that is applied to the process.

The Production Function

What we have described here is called a **production function**, which shows the relationship between input and output at various levels of each. With our other variables (land, capital, and managerial skills) held constant we get varying increases in outputs as we employ additional cooks. Total output increases rapidly at first, then more slowly in proportion to additional inputs. This is a common pattern in almost all production situations in the short run whenever the input of one variable factor is increased while the others are held constant.

 Key Concept: A production function shows the rate of increase in output from varying the level of inputs used.

This is shown in more detail in Figure 6-1. If we assume that a typical firm increases production by employing additional workers while holding all other inputs constant, then it can expect that its output pattern will go through different stages as shown in the upper panel, which depicts a typical production function.

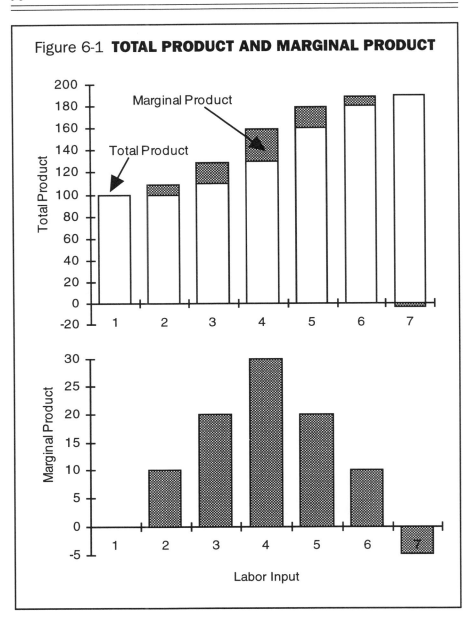

Figure 6-1 **TOTAL PRODUCT AND MARGINAL PRODUCT**

At first as additional labor inputs are employed output increases at an increasing rate but then begins to increase at a decreasing rate. This is shown more clearly by the marginal product curve in the lower panel. The *extra* products produced by each additional worker peaks at Point A and then begins to decrease. Throughout this stage average product per worker increases.

Then after Point B total product still increases but at a diminishing rate. Marginal product per worker continues to decrease until it reaches zero at Point C. Note that because the marginal product is less than the average, the average product curve begins to decline.

Finally, total product peaks at Point C, where absolute diminishing returns set in. Marginal product becomes negative, meaning that employing more workers is *decreasing* total production as they get in each other's way. At this point average product is declining rapidly.

Having such information tells a business firm a lot about the physical relationship between inputs and the resulting output in a physical engineering sense. But unless money values are attached to the costs of the inputs and prices are attached to the value of the output production function, analysis merely measures efficiency and productivity. (In Chapter 7 we apply these tools to a more practical problem—the question of how many inputs should be employed to maximize profits.) A more common and convenient way of analyzing the behavior of output related to input is to measure costs per unit of output. The two methods, as we shall see, are directly related. So, it is important to remember that a production function measures the level of a firm's output as inputs are increased.

COSTS FROM THE OUTPUT SIDE

Now that we understand the input view of the production process (that is, the production function), it will be easier to grasp the theory behind the more commonly used cost curve analysis, where costs are analyzed from the output perspective. Costs viewed from the output perspective are merely a mirror image of costs as seen from the input side.

The first and perhaps most important point is that *output curves are exactly the opposite of input curves*. This is illustrated in Figure 6-2. When physical output per unit of input is rising, the cost per unit of output is falling, and vice versa. If average output per unit is falling as units of input are added, then costs per unit are rising. Therefore, the total cost curve (in output terms) takes the opposite shape from the total product curve (in input terms). The same holds true for the average and marginal curves, which are derived from the total curve.

To understand this important concept, compare the average product and average cost curves shown in Figure 6-2b. Note that as the firm begins to increase production its efficiency (output per unit of input) improves. Because of this increase in efficiency, its costs per unit of output decline. That is, as the average product curve is rising, the average cost curve is falling. So the two curves move in opposite directions. Eventually the firm reaches its maximum efficiency (at the top of the average product curve or the bottom of the

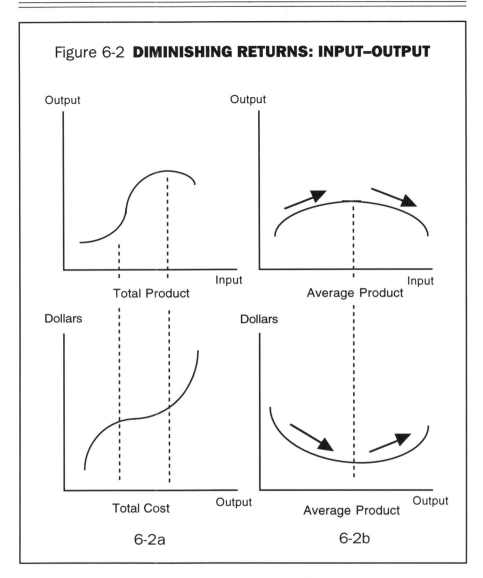

Figure 6-2 **DIMINISHING RETURNS: INPUT–OUTPUT**

Total Product

Average Product

Total Cost

Average Product

6-2a

6-2b

average cost curve); after that, output per unit of input begins to decline and the average product curve turns downward. For the same reason, costs per unit of input begin to rise, and the average cost curve turns upward.

So, to repeat the original point, average product curves and average cost curves take opposite shapes as production is increased. When output per unit of input is increasing, costs per unit of output are falling. When output begins to fall, costs begin to rise. In addition, cost curves have some special characteristics that we need to examine.

THE COST CURVES

All firms have several basic kinds of costs to consider, total and average fixed costs and total and average variable costs, plus marginal costs—the cost of producing one extra unit. They have quite different characteristics, but all are crucial for business firms that want to produce at a level consistent with profit maximization.

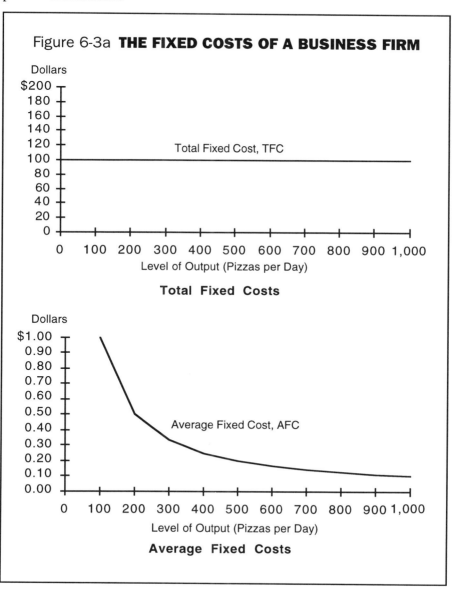

Figure 6-3a **THE FIXED COSTS OF A BUSINESS FIRM**

Total and Average Fixed Costs

Total **fixed costs** stay the same regardless of fluctuations in the level of output. For example, a factory would stay the same size (in the short run) and require the same upkeep no matter how much its production level varies. Fixed costs include such items as insurance and real estate taxes, which (as shown in

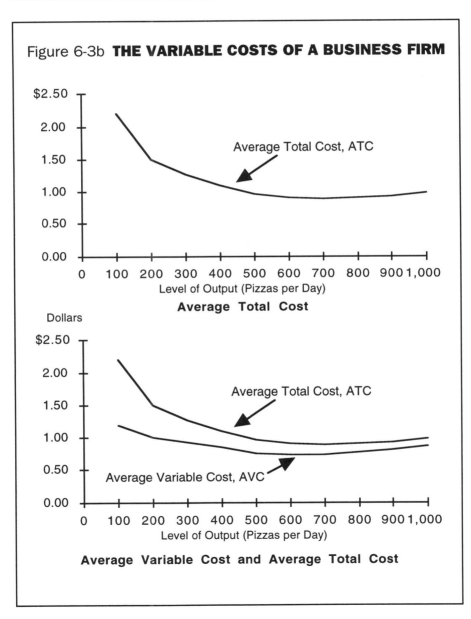

Figure 6-3b **THE VARIABLE COSTS OF A BUSINESS FIRM**

Figure 6-3a) remain the same at all levels of output. Fixed costs are some-times called "Sunday costs," because they are the costs that have to be paid even on Sunday, when the business may be closed.

 Key Concept: Fixed costs are a firm's costs that must be paid even if the firm is not producing.

Average Fixed Costs

When spread over a large range of production, fixed costs (total fixed costs/quantity) tend to become smaller and smaller in terms of the percentage that fixed costs per unit take of total costs as output increases. Eventually, they become relatively insignificant. This is shown in Figure 6-3a. In other words, average fixed costs are total fixed costs / quantity of output. In terms of cost per unit of output they become smaller as output increases.

Average Variable Costs

Variable costs are quite another matter. A firm can do little about fixed costs once it is in operation, but all other costs can be varied according to production goals and economic conditions. This is particularly true of labor and to a lesser extent of machinery, and other equipment. As we have seen, because of early efficiencies and later diminishing returns, output per unit of input increases at a faster rate at first and then more slowly. It logically fol-lows, then, that average costs decrease in the earlier stages of production, reach a minimum point, and then begin to increase. This is because costs per unit of output are falling as long as each additional worker (who is getting the same wage as every other worker) is producing more output. These relation-ships are shown in Figure 6-3b. To repeat: **average variable costs** are total variable costs / output. They decrease at first, reach a minimum point, then begin to increase, reflecting the law of diminishing returns.

 Key Concept: Average variable costs are total variable costs divided by units of output.

Average Total Costs

Combining the two curves (AFC and AVC) gives us the average total cost (ATC) curve, which, if it can be calculated, is very important data to any firm. Average total cost is the sum of average variable costs and average fixed costs at any level of output. This is shown in Figure 6-3b. Managers obviously need to know their most efficient level of production, that is, the lowest point on their average total cost curve, and at what point their costs will begin to

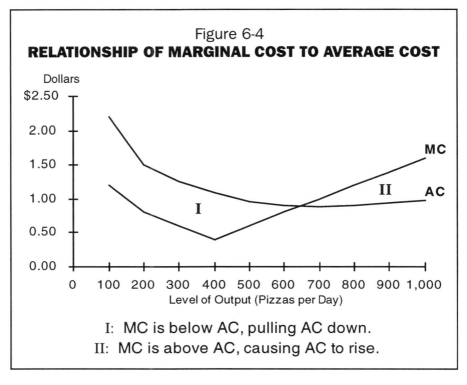

Figure 6-4
RELATIONSHIP OF MARGINAL COST TO AVERAGE COST

I: MC is below AC, pulling AC down.
II: MC is above AC, causing AC to rise.

rise, although, as we shall see, maximizing efficiency and maximizing profits are two different issues. Again, average total costs are total costs (fixed and variable) / output. They decline in early stages of production and then begin to increase.[2]

 Key Concept: Average total costs are the sum of average variable costs and average fixed costs at any level of output.

Marginal Costs

Another component of cost analysis is the **marginal cost** curve, which is logically related to the average cost and the total cost curves. As output is increased there is a specific cost involved in producing one additional unit of the product. Because efficiency increases at first and then eventually decreases,

---

[2]   Average total cost data also provides a shorthand way of calculating total cost. Since TC / Q = ATC, it follows that ATC x Q = TC.

the marginal (extra) cost of producing additional units follows the same pattern. Marginal costs per unit decrease and then rise.

 Key Concept: Marginal cost is the extra cost involved in producing one additional unit.

Marginal costs relate to average costs in the sense that, as shown in Figure 6-4, any time the extra cost per unit is less than the average the average is falling. Any time the marginal cost is higher than the average, the average cost is rising. This is not difficult to understand if you compare the concept to your grade average. If you consider your economics course as a marginal course, the grade you make in it will affect your grade average. If it is lower than your grade average, your average will be pulled down, if it is higher your average will be pulled up. When it comes to producing a product, the marginal and average costs involved in the process are related in the

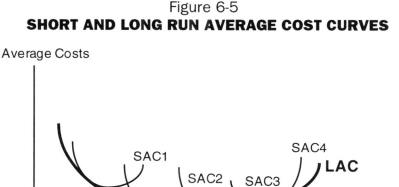

Figure 6-5
SHORT AND LONG RUN AVERAGE COST CURVES

Average Costs

SAC1 SAC2 SAC3 SAC4 **LAC**

Output

Each plant has its own "U" shaped average cost curve. As larger plants are built they are more efficient and have lower average costs. Eventually, however, the firm runs into decreasing returns and costs begin to rise.

same way. If the additional cost of producing another unit is higher than the average up to that point then the average cost is rising; if it is less, average cost is falling.

SHORT RUN VERSUS LONG RUN

We have been assuming throughout this chapter that all firms are small and operate with a fixed plant size in the short run. In other words, they cannot enlarge their physical facilities quickly enough to affect the shape of their average cost curves. In reality, of course, as economies develop and production levels increase, business firms do enlarge the scale of their operations and (up to a certain point) become more efficient.

This means (as shown in Figure 6-5) that **long-run average cost** (LAC) **curves** are merely a combination of a series of short-run average cost (SAC) curves over time. Each time a firm enlarges, it tends to become more efficient; that is, it sees a lowering of average costs per unit. If this didn't happen, expanding production capacity wouldn't make any sense. But at some point, as the firm becomes too large to manage and control efficiently or runs into scarcity of resources, the average cost curve begins to rise. This, then, becomes a question of economies of scale.

 Key Concept: Long-run average cost curves are the combination of short-run average cost curves as measured over a longer time period.

Economies of Scale

The U-shaped cost curves we have been examining are based on the assumption of diminishing returns to output, as one factor input is varied while others are held constant. That is, however, a short-run assumption that—while it has many practical applications—doesn't necessarily apply to longer-run considerations in which all factors are variable. Under such conditions all business firms encounter what is called **economies of scale** of several different types. Economies of scale are the forces that cause average total costs to decline or remain constant as production is increased.

 Key Concept: Economies of scale exist when all inputs are increased and output increases by a larger percentage.

One possibility is *constant returns to scale*, which is not uncommon in some industries over a wide range of production as firms take advantage of mass production techniques. In a constant returns-to-scale situation, as shown in Figure 6-7(a), a firm or industry may be able to expand production considerably and yet never experience increasing costs.

More common is the existence of *economies of scale* shown in Figure 6-6, where as firms and industries grow larger, they become more efficient. Large firms can afford more specialists and more computerized equipment, and can

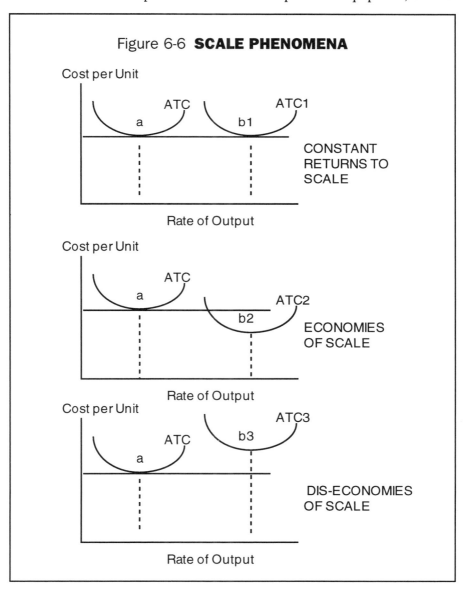

Figure 6-6 **SCALE PHENOMENA**

utilize mass production techniques that make them more efficient than small firms.

In other industries *dis-economies of scale* may exist where expansion of output (Figure 6-6) may soon encounter forces that cause costs to increase. This often occurs when resources become scarce or depleted or when supporting infrastructure becomes congested. In recent years, for example, the airline industry has expanded considerably, but the number of airports available has remained roughly the same. The result is higher costs, congested airports, and longer waits at the gate.

In any of these cases it is economies of scale over the long run that occur when all inputs are varied that count. This is not the same situation faced by a firm varying one input and encountering the law of diminishing returns.

SUMMARY

✓ What is commonly called the theory of production deals primarily with the analysis of the production process and its related costs.

✓ Business firm production and costs can be analyzed from two different perspectives: The input side and the output side.

✓ If we consider production from the input side, we are concerned with the relationship of inputs of the factors of production (land, labor, capital, and know-how) to the amount of output we get from them.

✓ Economic and engineering studies show that when the inputs of some factors—such as land or the size of plant—are fixed in the short-run, then output increases in proportion to inputs and then increases at a decreasing rate.

✓ When we analyze production from the perspective of costs per unit of output the same thing happens in reverse. When output from additional input is increasing, then average costs per unit of output are decreasing. As output increases more slowly, costs begin to increase. Therefore, average cost curves tend to be U-shaped.

✓ Most business firms, especially those in manufacturing, cannot quickly change the scale (size) of their plants. Therefore, most microeconomic analysis of the firm assumes that short-run conditions prevail.

✓ In the long-run, the size of a plant can be changed. Long-run cost curves are, in effect, a series of short-run curves. Since inefficiencies tend to develop as firms become very large, the long-run costs are assumed to take a similar U-shape, but somewhat flatter.

NEW VOCABULARY

productivity	average fixed costs (AFC)
law of diminishing returns	average variable costs (AVC)
production function	average total costs (ATC)
total fixed costs (TFC)	marginal costs (MC)
total variable costs (TVC)	long-run average costs (LRAC)
total costs (TC)	economies of scale

QUESTIONS FOR REVIEW

1. How does the Law of Diminishing Returns explain the shape of a production function?

2. What is the relationship between total product, average product, and marginal product?

3. What is the relationship between the total cost curve and the law of diminishing returns?

4. What is the difference between total fixed costs and total variable costs?

5. What is the relationship between marginal costs and average costs?

6. At what point is a firm producing at its maximum economic efficiency? Why?

7. What is the economic meaning of the difference between short-run and long-run? Can you give an example?

8. When a firm is experiencing dis-economies of scale, what is happening in terms of its production costs? What should it do?

Chapter 7

PERFECT COMPETITION

LEARNING OBJECTIVES

In this chapter we examine the various ways that different sectors of the economy are organized. We begin with perfect competition as a idealized model and then look at variations from it, such as oligopoly and monopoly. Specifically, we look at:

- ✓ how competition is the driving force of the capitalist system.
- ✓ the basic characteristics and assumptions of perfect competition.
- ✓ how the analysis of costs and revenues helps business firms maximize profits.
- ✓ why, when a firm's marginal costs equal its marginal revenues, its profits are maximized.
- ✓ the relationship between one firm's marginal cost curve and the market supply curve.
- ✓ how perfect competition would force all firms into long-run equilibrium.

INTRODUCTION

Now we begin to look at the different market structures that function in most capitalist economies. We start with trying to understand what the world would look like if it were organized around an idealized state of affairs called perfect competition. Then we learn more about the shape of supply and demand curves, cost and revenue curves, and how, by analyzing them carefully, firms can maximize their profits. That will help us better understand the theory behind the supply curve and why it usually takes an upward path. Throughout this chapter we will assume a perfectly competitive market structure exists, keeping in mind that there are others.

Other Market Structures

The perfectly competitive market model has a certain theoretical elegance, and it has a number of useful applications—as we shall see shortly. However, there is an important caveat to keep in mind before we proceed. Perfectly competitive firms make up only a small portion of the U.S. and other free market economies of the world. Most of the U.S. economy is organized around imperfectly competitive market structures in the sense that most firms are big enough to have some influence over their selling price.

The polar opposite of perfect competition is *monopoly*, where the firm has control over price because it is the only seller. Like the 800-pound gorilla, it can do pretty much what it wants to or, at least, it could if it were not regulated by the government as are most monopolies. The utility companies are the most common example of this market structure, which we will want to examine in the following chapter.

In between these polar opposites are the *monopolistic competitors*— mostly retail outlets—that enjoy some monopoly power over price, but also face stiff competition

Even more important are large corporations called *oligopolies* that dominate much of the world economic landscape. Many industries, such as the auto industry, steel, communications, computers, and transportation, are controlled by only a few giant firms wielding considerable power over their markets and market prices. These firms compete, but not the same way as in the world of perfect competition if it existed. They, too, are the subject of the next chapter.

Having alerted you to some of the more important departures from the idealized world of perfect competition, we continue to develop the theory. In the process, we will learn how to apply some useful new tools, some of which apply equally to all market structures. We will then be able to see why the idealized perfectly competitive model is a useful gauge by which to measure other—less competitive—market structures.

Perfect Competition

A perfectly competitive world is one in which the laws of supply and demand that we have examined in earlier chapters would explain virtually everything related to economic activity. Perfect competition is easy to understand if you visualize all economic transactions taking place in an auction setting. Prices are flexible and based on what people bid for whatever is being auctioned. The demand is determined by what people in the audience are willing to pay, and the product is sold to the highest bidder. The supply is determined by what sellers bring to the market to be sold at auction.

If everything we purchased was sold in an auction setting then perfect competition would exist. In the modern world the agricultural commodities markets and the stock markets are the closest examples of perfect competition. Prices in those markets are literally determined in an auction setting. But in most cases we don't go into a store and bargain over the price of things we want to purchase. Instead, we pay the stated price or we don't buy. Competition enters the process in a more subtle way, depending on the power of buyers and sellers to control and maintain the selling price of the product. These subtleties will be examined in the following chapter. For now we assume the economy operates in an auction setting, where buyers compete with each other as they bid for products offered in the market.

Under **perfect competition** the equilibrium point at which supply and demand curves intersect represents a state in which producers are as well off as they possibly can be, selling their products at the highest possible price consistent with their costs. This gives them an income equal to their opportunity costs. Consumers also share in this blissful state, because by competing with each other they are able to buy what they want at a price consistent with their desires—their utility schedules, assuming they have sufficient incomes to do so.

 Key Concept: Perfect competition is a situation in which all economic transactions are conducted in an auction setting. Neither sellers nor buyers can influence prices.

Characteristics of Perfect Competition

For us to develop a model of perfectly competitive markets we must make a number of assumptions. The most important assumption is that perfectly competitive firms are **price takers** in the sense that they are assumed to be so small that they have no influence over market price; they simply have to take it, whatever the market says it is. Many small businesses are in this situation. The most common example is in agriculture, where farmers can sell all they produce at the market price. The price may vary every day, but whatever it is, the farmer must take it in order to sell, say, wheat. A similar situation exists for any product sold in an organized commodity market—ranging from gold to pork bellies. Producers can sell as much as they wish, so long as they are willing to accept the going price.

 Key Concept: Price takers are firms that are so small in a perfectly competitive industry they have no influence over the market price.

Beyond the price-taking assumption a number of other specific requirements must be met for a market to be considered perfectly competitive:

1. There must be a large number of both buyers and sellers in the market, none large enough to influence the market price. If one buyer or seller is large enough to withhold enough of the product to cause a shortage, then the market price will be affected and perfect competition will no longer exist.

2. All products sold in the market must be homogeneous, that is, similar if not exactly the same. Given certain technical specifications, all wheat is wheat, for example, and gold is gold. All producers of a product sell exactly the same thing.

3. There must be no barriers to entering or exiting the market. If it is difficult to enter the market—say, large outlays for factories or equipment are needed—then existing firms could influence the market price.

4. Both buyers and sellers must have complete knowledge of market price information. If perfect knowledge of prices exists, then no buyer would ever pay more than the market price, nor could any seller ever sell for more than that price.

The Demand Curve

If all these conditions prevail in a price-taker setting, then the perfectly competitive firm faces a perfectly elastic—horizontal—demand curve. That is, it can sell all it can produce at the market price. This is a theoretically subtle point that merits careful consideration. The market demand curve for any product is, as we have seen, generally downward sloping, signifying that the market price must be lowered if more is to be sold. But since no small firm is large enough to influence the market price, and all firms *are* small, then no one firm can raise or lower the price. In other words, for example, if the market price of wheat is $3 a bushel, then wheat farmers can sell all they want at that price. So for them the demand curve for wheat is horizontal. (This is demonstrated in Figure 7-1.) If the market forces of supply and demand set the price of wheat at $3 a bushel then wheat farmers will sell all they can produce for a *cost* less than $3. So, while the market demand curve slopes downward, the demand curve for one individual farmer is horizontal. The farmer is, therefore, left with the relatively simple problem of producing the appropriate level of output at the lowest cost in order to maximize profits.

To repeat this important point: Perfect competitors are so small in relation to the size of the market that they cannot influence the market. Therefore, they must take the market price. This means their demand curve is horizontal.

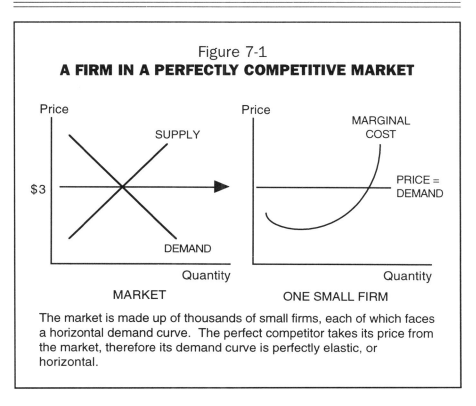

Figure 7-1
A FIRM IN A PERFECTLY COMPETITIVE MARKET

MARKET

ONE SMALL FIRM

The market is made up of thousands of small firms, each of which faces a horizontal demand curve. The perfect competitor takes its price from the market, therefore its demand curve is perfectly elastic, or horizontal.

TOTAL, AVERAGE, AND MARGINAL COSTS

As we saw in the previous chapter, a firm's cost profile is the opposite of its production function. When output per unit of input is increasing (proportionately), then cost per unit of output is decreasing. When additional units of input begin to yield less additional output, then unit costs (on average) begin to increase. This is because the firm's size is fixed in the short run or because only one input is varied while the others are held constant. Marginal costs reflect this as they decline faster than average costs. Knowledge of this data helps a firm minimize its costs. Cost information, however, is only part of the picture. To be sure, firms are interested in minimizing costs, but they are more interested in maximizing profits. To understand why, revenues must also be analyzed.

Total and Marginal Revenues

Under perfect competition, revenue from each unit of sales is equal to price. Since the firm can sell all it can produce at the market price its **marginal revenue** curve—the additional revenue it receives from selling one more unit—is a straight line, horizontal, reflecting perfect elasticity of demand. And, as a practical matter, many firms that are competitive to some degree face a similar situation in the short-run over their relevant range of production and sales because they don't change their prices every day. That is, a wheat farmer's marginal revenue is equal to the price of each additional

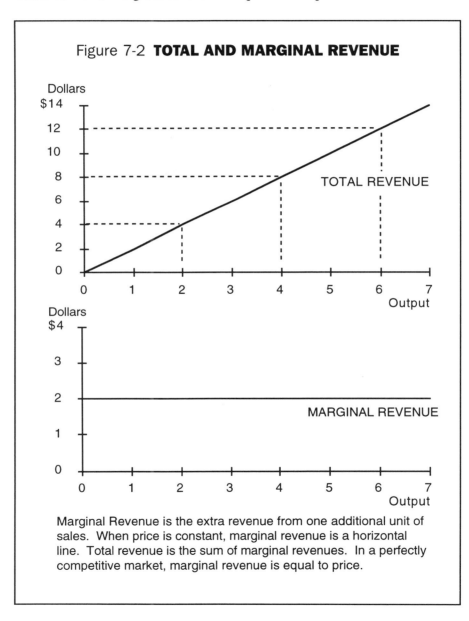

Figure 7-2 **TOTAL AND MARGINAL REVENUE**

Marginal Revenue is the extra revenue from one additional unit of sales. When price is constant, marginal revenue is a horizontal line. Total revenue is the sum of marginal revenues. In a perfectly competitive market, marginal revenue is equal to price.

bushel of wheat sold. The marginal revenue of a pizza parlor is the price of each additional pizza sold. And **total revenue** is the sum of the price of all additional units sold. This means that, as shown in Figure 7-2, a firm's total revenue curve is not a curve at all, but a straight line sloping upward and to the right because the price of each unit is the same.

Key Concept: Marginal revenue is the additional revenue received from the sale of one unit of product.

Key Concept: Total revenue is the sum of marginal revenue, or price times quantity sold.

Total Revenue versus Total Cost

If a firm has complete data on revenues and costs, the next step is to calculate total revenues (TR) minus total costs (TC) at various levels of production. The difference between the two (TR − TC) is **total profit**. Since we assume that all firms want to maximize profits, their objective is to produce at a level where the difference between total revenues and total costs is the greatest. The upper portion of Figure 7-3 shows the total cost and total revenue profile for a typical competitive firm. With a constant given price taken from the market, the total revenue curve is a straight line sloping upward and to the right from the origin. However, because of the law of diminishing returns total costs increase at a declining rate at first and then increase rapidly. At the production level where the vertical distance (points A to B) between total cost and total revenue is greatest, profit is maximized.

Key Concept: Total profit is total revenue minus total cost.

MARGINAL COST AND MARGINAL REVENUE

It is also possible to determine the point of maximum profit by comparing marginal cost (MC) per unit of output to marginal revenue (MR) per unit of sales. Since under perfect competition the firm has no control over price but, instead, simply sells at a price determined by the market, the price of the product and the extra revenue obtained from selling one unit are identical. And, as we have seen, the marginal revenue curve is therefore a straight horizontal line, the same at every level of output.

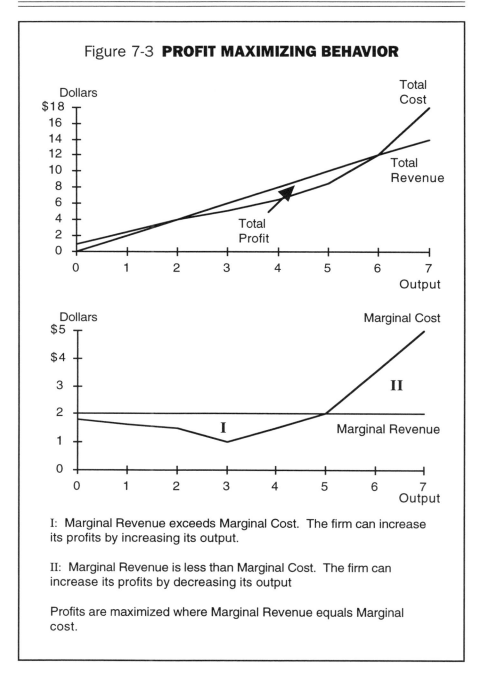

Figure 7-3 **PROFIT MAXIMIZING BEHAVIOR**

I: Marginal Revenue exceeds Marginal Cost. The firm can increase its profits by increasing its output.

II: Marginal Revenue is less than Marginal Cost. The firm can increase its profits by decreasing its output

Profits are maximized where Marginal Revenue equals Marginal cost.

The relationship between these two curves (MC and MR) is perhaps the most important information a firm can have, because it enables the firm to determine with some certainty the level of output that will yield the highest level of profit—given a certain price. This is shown in the lower portion of Figure 7-3.

So long as marginal revenue is greater than marginal cost it is profitable for the firm to increase production, since the return on the most recent unit sold is greater than the cost of producing it. The important thing to remember here is that PROFIT IS MAXIMIZED WHERE MR = MC. But at any point beyond where MR = MC, the firm is incurring a loss on each additional unit produced, assuming that the market price does not increase.

This important concept is worth reviewing. Look again at Figure 7-3. In the lower panel a typically perfect competitive firm's marginal revenue and marginal cost curves are shown. Now consider its profit maximizing strategy at different levels of output. When it is producing and selling 3 units its marginal costs (of producing the third unit) are less than the marginal revenue it receives from selling the product at the market price. Should it then try to produce and sell more units? Yes, so long as the extra costs involved are less than the revenue received.

In this example, when production is increased to 4 units, the cost of producing the 4th exactly equals the revenue received. At that point (where MR = MC) its profits are maximized. (Note that in the upper panel the vertical distance between total cost and total revenue is the greatest.) Now, should it try to produce and sell any more units? No, because if it increases production to 5 units the cost of producing the 5th unit exceeds the revenue received from selling it. It takes a loss on that unit and its total profits begin to decrease.

Therefore, at any level of production where marginal costs are less than marginal revenues it makes sense to increase production because a profit is being made on each additional unit sold. When marginal costs equal marginal revenues it's time to stop producing additional units (in a given time period). Producing at an output level beyond the point where MR = MC is clearly not rational because a loss is being incurred on each additional unit sold.

This is why one of the most important laws of microeconomics is that *firms maximize profits when marginal revenue equals marginal cost.*

A COMPOSITE PICTURE

What we have been doing so far is analyzing the characteristics of a typical small business firm by looking at its separate component parts. In the previous chapter we looked at the physical production process. First we analyzed the input side—the behavior of the production function. Then we analyzed the same process from the output side by studying cost curves and how they are derived. Then in this chapter we have seen how firms attempt to maximize profits by producing at a level where marginal costs = marginal revenue.

Now we can put these tools together in a way that presents a composite picture of the firm using only three key curves: marginal cost, marginal revenue, and average cost. This is shown in Figure 7-4.

The data necessary to calculate profits (or losses) is total revenue and total cost. In Figure 7-4 total revenue (price x quantity sold) is the rectangle OBCE. Total cost is the rectangle OADE. This is calculated from the AC curve, that is, AC x Q = TC. And total profit is the difference between the two, or rectangle ABCD. Note that even though the firm only produced up to the point that MR = MC (output OE), it still has profits. Any increase in production beyond that point will reduce profits. You should, by now, be able to explain why.

Figure 7-4
PROFIT MAXIMIZATION UNDER PERFECT COMPETITION

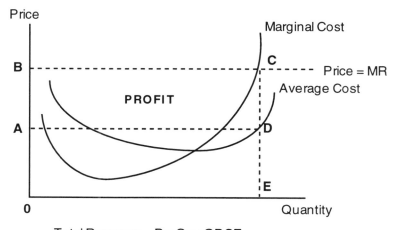

Total Revenue = P x Q or OBCE
Total Cost = AO x Q or OADE
Profit = TR - TC or OBCE - OADE = ABCD

Profit is maximized when MR = MC. Total profit is total revenue minus total costs. Alternatively, profit can be viewed as price times the quantity sold (the rectangle OBCE) minus average cost times the quantity sold (rectangle OADE), hence profits are represented by the rectangle ABCD.

Marginal Cost and the Supply Curve

Now we can demonstrate more rigorously why we said earlier that supply curves always slope upward—which may have seemed simplistic at the time. Assume in Figure 7-5 that a market disturbance, such as a change in tastes, has the effect of raising price from P1 to P2. This causes a very direct and predictable response by the firm. To maximize its profits the firm will move up along its marginal cost curve, increasing production from Q1 to Q2 until the point where MR once again equals MC. The effect on total production, as all firms begin to do the same, is to increase quantity from Q1 to Q2. Therefore, for all practical purposes, *a firm's supply curve and its marginal cost curve are the same thing* because market supply curves are a summation of many small firms' supply curves.

In other words, all that supply curves tell us is that business firms will increase the quantity supplied as the price increases. Since all firms attempt to produce at an output level where marginal costs equal marginal revenue (that is, price) then it follows that they will expand output when price rises and reduce output when the market price falls. This merely confirms our earlier statement that supply is a function of price [S = f (P)], but now we can see why.

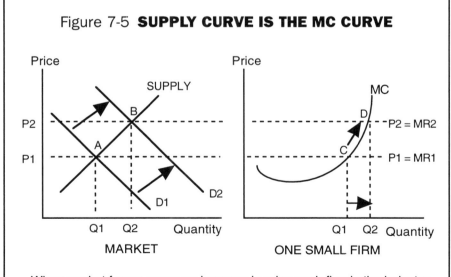

Figure 7-5 **SUPPLY CURVE IS THE MC CURVE**

When market forces cause an increase in price each firm in the industry responds by increasing production until it reachs its new profit maximization point — where its marginal cost equals the new higher price.

SHORT-RUN PROFITS VERSUS LONG-RUN EQUILIBRIUM

In the examples we have examined so far, all of our firms have been earning substantial profits. Under conditions of perfect competition, however, this can happen only in the short run. The reason stems from a natural human tendency. In an industry that is easy to get into ("easy market entry," as economists call it), if one firm is making profits, others will want to enter the market and make profits too. As more and more firms come into the industry, supply increases and prices are pushed downward. This is shown in Figure 7-6.

The effect of increased supply in the overall market on one individual firm is to force it to move down its marginal cost curve, eventually to the point where its marginal cost, marginal revenue, and average costs are all equal. At that point no economic profits exist. All firms in the industry earn only "normal" profits, which are equal to their opportunity costs. Note also that at this level of output each firm is operating at a level where its efficiency in terms of costs is maximized or, put differently, where its costs are at the lowest possible level—at the bottom of its average cost curve. Now no additional firms

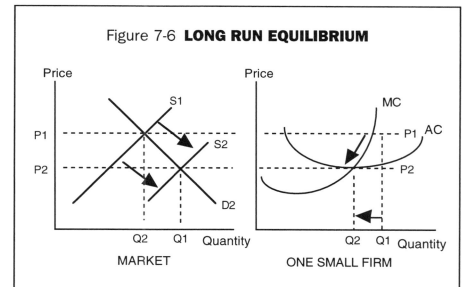

Figure 7-6 LONG RUN EQUILIBRIUM

MARKET

ONE SMALL FIRM

As more firms enter the industry and competition pushes price down, existing firms are forced to decrease production to the point that marginal cost equals marginal revenue (price) at the bottom of their average cost curve. When MR (P) = MC = AC profits are reduced to a level equal to opportunity costs and the industry is in long run equilibrium.

will be interested in coming into the market because no economic profits exist. Therefore, the industry is in **long-run equilibrium**, and prices will be stable until some variables outside the model (such as a change in tastes or incomes) come along to increase or decrease the level of demand or supply.

Key Concept: In long-run equilibrium, under perfect competition marginal revenue (price), marginal costs and average costs are all equal.

COMPETITION AND EFFICIENCY

The reason the perfectly competitive model is so attractive to economists and others is that if it existed throughout the economy then the economy would operate at maximum efficiency to everyone's best interest. Producers would sell at a price equal to their lowest average costs and earn normal profits equal to their opportunity costs; no one then would have any incentive to do anything other than what they were presently doing. Consumers would be able to buy at that same price, which is the price at which they would be able to maximize their utility (satisfaction) per dollar of expenditure.

In this ideal world of perfect competition, the problem of allocating resources is also resolved—by the forces of the market. If in any industry resources or products are priced above minimum average costs, society will vote to shift resources to that industry because there are economic profits to be earned. For that same reason, profits cannot exist for long in a perfectly competitive market.

Unfortunately, the idealized model of perfect competition remains just that—an idealized model. It doesn't exist in pure form anywhere in the U.S. economy. Yet it remains the ideal of capitalist perfection, the model by which all other models and, indeed, all other theoretical depictions of economic reality are judged. Its practical importance is found in approximations of it and in its ability to help us understand the departures from it, which we need to do now.

SUMMARY

✓ Under perfect competition the equilibrium point at which supply and demand curves intersect is a state in which producers are as well off as they can possibly be, selling their products at the highest possible price. Consumers are able to buy what they want at a price consistent with their desires—their utility schedules—and their incomes.

✓ In addition to perfect competition there are (at least) three other market structures: (1) monopoly, (2) monopolistic competition, and (3) oligopoly. Each of these is a form of imperfect competition.

✓ Perfectly competitive firms are price takers; they are so small that they have no influence over market price.

✓ A perfectly competitive market has the following characteristics: (1) there is a large number of both buyers and sellers, none large enough to influence the market price; (2) all products sold in the market are homogeneous, that is, similar if not exactly the same; (3) there are no barriers to entering or exiting the market; and (4) both buyers and sellers have complete knowledge of market information.

✓ Under perfect competition, revenue per unit of sales is equal to price. The additional revenue the firm receives from selling one more unit is its marginal revenue. The competitive firm's marginal revenue curve is a horizontal straight line. Thus, the total revenue curve is not really a curve but a straight line sloping upward and to the right.

✓ The difference between total revenues (TR) and total costs (TC) is total profit (TR - TC = TP). Since all firms presumably want to maximize their profit, they seek to produce at a level of output where the difference (vertical distance) between TR and TC is greatest.

✓ It is also possible to determine the output level that would maximize profit from the relationship between marginal cost (MC) and marginal revenue (MR). The level of production that maximizes profit is the point at which marginal revenue equals marginal cost (MR = MC).

✓ In the short-run, perfectly competitive firms can earn economic profits; the existence of economic profits will, however, attract other firms in the long run. The entry of additional firms into a perfectly competitive market will increase market supply.

✓ Increased supply will lower prices. This will force firms to move back down their marginal cost (supply) curves. Eventually, all firms will be forced to produce at the point where their MC = MR = AC (marginal cost equals marginal revenue equals average cost).

✓ Like all economic models, the model of perfect competition is a theoretical abstraction. Its primary purpose is to enable us to understand the rationale for competitive markets. In addition, it gives us a conceptual framework for a better understanding of other market structures.

NEW VOCABULARY

perfect competition   total profit
price takers   total revenues
marginal revenue   long-run equilibrium

QUESTIONS FOR REVIEW

1. What are the basic assumptions of perfect competition?
2. Why is the demand curve for perfect competitors horizontal?
3. In addition to perfect competition, what are the other three major market structures?
4. In a perfectly competitive firm what is the shape of the total cost curve? the average cost curve? and marginal cost curve?
5. In a perfectly competitive firm what is the shape of the total revenue and marginal revenue curves?
6. At what level of output will a perfectly competitive firm maximize profits? Explain.
7. Why does the summation of all firms' marginal cost curves add up to the market supply curve?
8. What determines the break-even point for a perfectly competitive firm?
9. Under what conditions should a perfectly competitive firm shut down production?
10. Theoretically, how does perfect competition bring about efficiency in the long run?

Chapter 8
IMPERFECT COMPETITION

LEARNING OBJECTIVES

In this chapter we will learn:

- ✓ Why monopoly is the polar opposite of perfect competition.
- ✓ Why monopolies are not necessarily bad.
- ✓ How monopolies can set their prices and output levels to maximize profits.
- ✓ Why many industries are made up of firms that are partly monopolies and partly competitors.
- ✓ How advertising affects our buying habits.
- ✓ How markets and industries that are dominated by only several firms—called oligopolies—operate.
- ✓ How such firms are interdependent and how that affects their pricing strategies.
- ✓ Why the large oligopolies rarely lower the price of their product.
- ✓ How the oligopolies compete with each other for market share.
- ✓ Why it is so difficult for a small firm to compete with large, established firms.
- ✓ How foreign competition has changed the way in which large corporations do business.

INTRODUCTION

In this chapter our primary objective is to continue our excursion through the different market structures found in capitalistic economies. Here we focus on the monopoly, which is the polar opposite of the competitive model we have studied so far. We will see that monopolies play an important and quite legitimate role in the U.S. economy. Also, we shall see that monopoly doesn't necessarily equal big. Many of the small, seemingly competitive firms that we deal with daily—such as grocery stores and shoe stores—exhibit many characteristics of monopoly, although mixed with some healthy competition.

PURE COMPETITION VERSUS PURE MONOPOLY

As we have just seen, under pure competition a firm is assumed to be so small that nothing it does will affect the price for which it sells its product. It is, in effect, a price taker, since it must take its selling price from the market. The demand curve it faces, therefore, is horizontal and perfectly elastic. That is, a firm operating in a perfectly competitive market can sell all it wants at the market price. This is because it is so small that its actions do not affect the market.

On the other hand, a monopoly, which by definition is the only seller of a product, faces the market demand curve, which, as we have seen, generally slopes downward. That is, by virtue of being the only seller in the market a monopolist has the advantage of being able to have some control over the price; for which it sells its product. It is not, however, exempt from the law of demand. The monopolist therefore is a **price maker**. Assuming that demand is relatively stable, it can sell more only if it is willing to lower price. This has interesting theoretical and practical implications, as we shall see shortly.

 Key Concept: A price maker is a firm that has sufficient control over its market to be able to set its selling price and level of output to its advantage.

MONOPOLIES

Monopolies, then, are the polar opposite of perfect competitors. The characteristics of monopoly markets include the following:

1. There is one seller of a good or service.
2. The product is unique, and there are no close substitutes; buyers *must* buy the good or service from the monopolist.
3. The monopoly can exercise control over the price of the good/service, since it supplies the total quantity of the good/service. The firm has market power. This is opposed to the competitive firm, whose price is determined by the market and has no influence on the price of its product.
4. Monopolies usually exist because there are absolute barriers to entry into the market; no other firm can supply the product because of legal, technological, or geographical barriers.

5. The monopoly may or may not advertise.

Of course, situations where all of these conditions prevail are rather rare. Perfect or pure monopolies are found only in a few instances where competition is difficult, even irrational. These firms—called **natural monopolies**—are usually regulated if not owned by the local government, at least in the United States. The most common example is public utilities: electricity, gas, water, and telephone service. It is usually nonsensical for two companies to be competing for customers with separate telephone lines or with two sets of water pipes running down the same street.

 Key Concept: Natural monopolies are generally utilities such as electricity, gas, water, and telephone companies.

The word monopoly is often technically misused. We may hear certain large firms being called "monopolies" when in fact they are not at all. A monopoly must be the only seller of a product. This confusion exists because in many industries, such as the auto industry, there are only a few sellers. This makes some firms appear to be monopolies and—in fact—allows them to act much as if they were, so we need to make careful distinctions. In between the pure monopolist and the pure competitor is the monopolistic competitor, a subtle combination of both, and the oligopoly.

What distinguishes all these different models is the number of sellers, the degree of elasticity of demand for their products, and the extent to which substitutes are available. Even a pure monopoly does not face a perfectly inelastic demand curve because, in most cases, if its price becomes excessively high, consumers will begin to seek out substitutes. For example, in many less-developed countries where telephone service is relatively expensive, telegraphs and other ways of sending messages are common. So the telephone companies do not have complete control of the message communications market. Electric companies do not have a perfect monopoly over their market because there are some alternatives to electric power, although not many. And there are other examples.

What is significant here is that, like any firm, a monopoly wants to maximize its profits. If there are no social restrictions on its actions it can do so by setting its selling price as high as possible by restricting its output. To understand why, we have to examine more carefully the demand and marginal revenue conditions that prevail in a monopolistic market. They are quite different than those in a competitive market.

Demand And Marginal Revenue

First, let's take a simple model of the demand and marginal revenue curves for pure monopoly, say a cable TV company, as shown in Figure 8-1. Note that to increase the number of customers subscribing to its basic service the firm must lower price. This means that marginal revenue (the extra revenue gained from selling an additional unit) will always be less than price. Why? Because, since the firm sells its product to everyone at the same price, it must lower price on all units if it wants to increase sales.

Let's see how this works. If the local cable TV company is a monopoly (the only one in town) and wants to increase its revenues, it must lower its monthly subscription price. At a price of $20 it could find 100 households to sign up for the basic service. From that its total revenue would be $2000 a month. But its marketing studies show that if it lowered the price to $19, then another 100 households would sign up. Therefore, its total revenue would increase from $2000 to $3700, which makes lowering the price a sensible thing to do. Note, however, the subtleties of the situation, given that this is a monopoly.

Total revenues did increase, but the firm's marginal revenues are already beginning to decrease. When it lowered the price from $20 to $19 it couldn't simply lower price just for the second 100 subscribers but, instead, had to lower its price for all of its customers. So while it gained revenue from the new customers, it lost some revenue from the lower price it now has to charge its first 100 customers. (It gained $1800, but lost $200 in the process.) As that process continues, each time it lowers price it gains additional revenues from the new customers but loses from having to lower its current price for current subscribers.

Looked at in a different way its (average) marginal revenue falls faster than its (average) price per customer. (See Figure 8-1.) Because of this curious relationship between price and marginal revenue the monopoly faces a quite different situation than does the perfectly competitive firm that can sell all it wishes at the market price. This is because the monopoly for all practical purposes is the market in the sense that it faces the (downward sloping) market demand curve. Indeed, at some point (at 1100 customers in our example) the monopoly has reached the point where lowering price will not give it any additional revenue at all. This leaves the interesting question of: What is the level of sales the monopoly should strive for if it wants to maximize its profits? That question can only be answered when we know more about its cost picture.

Costs in Monopolistic Market Structures

As we have seen, monopolies are not exempt from the law of demand: they have to lower price to increase sales. By the same reasoning they are also not exempt from the law of increasing costs because they face short-run di-minishing returns to increasing inputs. That means their average total cost curves are U-shaped. In the early stages of production they decrease and then

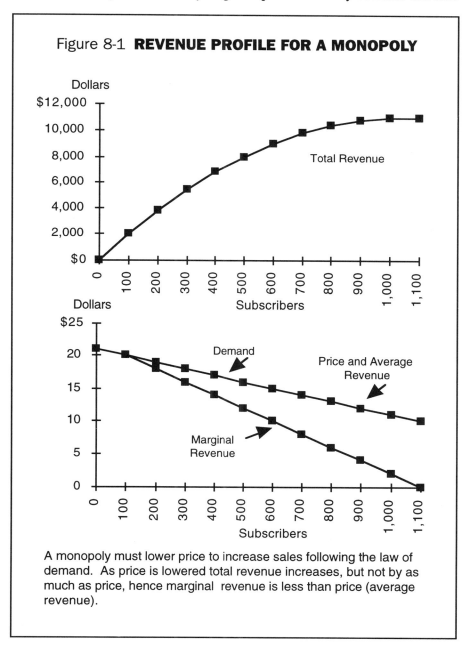

Figure 8-1 **REVENUE PROFILE FOR A MONOPOLY**

A monopoly must lower price to increase sales following the law of demand. As price is lowered total revenue increases, but not by as much as price, hence marginal revenue is less than price (average revenue).

begin to increase as diminishing returns set in. Therefore, in essence, their cost curves take the same shape as the perfect competitor's. And, by the same reasoning we studied in the previous chapter, monopolies maximize profits where their marginal revenue per unit equals their marginal cost per unit.

Note, however, that in a perfectly competitive situation marginal revenue is always equal to price, which means that when MR = MC profits are zero, equal to opportunity costs. But, since in monopoly marginal revenue is always less *than price*, a profit-maximizing monopolist will want to set its output level where MR = MC and then charge the highest price its demand curve will permit. This difference always yields a monopoly the highest possible profit—which usually also means that it will be producing at a level of output lower than its minimum average cost. The net result is that the monopoly charges higher prices and produces less than it would in a more competitive market environment.

This unusual situation is shown in Figure 8-2 where the cost curves for the local cable TV company are superimposed on its demand and revenue picture (from Figure 8-1). Its marginal revenue and marginal cost curves intersect at output level 800, which is the number of customers it needs to maximize profits. At that point its price is well above its average cost curve, yielding a tidy profit.[1] At any other level profits will be smaller. The reason is the same as for any other firm. If the firm produces at levels where marginal revenue is more than marginal cost, it is losing potential profits, so it should increase production to the point where MR = MC. If it increases output beyond that point, then it is costing more to produce those additional units than the firm is getting in additional revenues per unit, and this is clearly irrational from the monopoly's point of view, because it lowers its profits. So, a monopolist has the option of setting its level of output where MR = MC—where profits are maximized.

In perfect competition the firm can only make economic profits if there is a temporary market disequilibrium, but since the imperfect competitor has control over price it can and will set its level of production where it almost always makes economic profits. The amount of these profits depends on the degree of control the firm has over its selling price. This, in turn, depends on the degree of elasticity of demand for its products, that is, the extent to which substitutes are available.

Regulation

All this helps us understand why pure monopolies are regulated. If you were a government economist studying how to regulate the cable TV industry

---

[1] Remember that TR = P x Q and TC = AC x Q; the difference—TR - TC equals total profit.

we just analyzed so as to eliminate economic profits, what level of output would you recommend? You would want it to produce at the point where price equals average costs (where TR - TC = zero.) At this point investors receive only a normal return on their investment, output is greater than the unregulated monopoly would choose, and price is lower.

Needless to say, attempts at regulation result in some heated debates between economists representing the utility companies and those employed by the various public regulatory agencies. But utility rate-setting hearings are one of the better examples of how microeconomic theory can be applied to practical problems. The essence of what is happening when pure monopolies are regulated is that the government is trying to make them behave as if they were perfect competitors, producing at a level where their price equals their average costs, which is where economic profits would be zero, or equal to

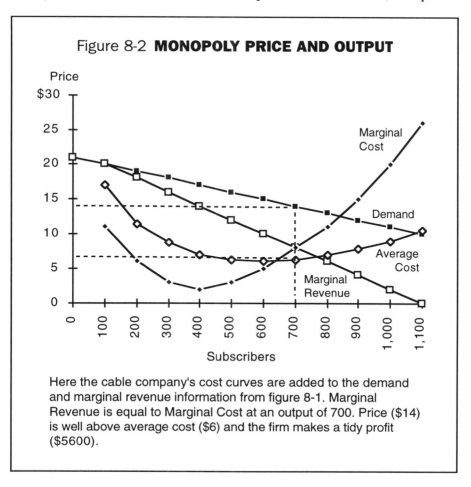

Figure 8-2 **MONOPOLY PRICE AND OUTPUT**

Here the cable company's cost curves are added to the demand and marginal revenue information from figure 8-1. Marginal Revenue is equal to Marginal Cost at an output of 700. Price ($14) is well above average cost ($6) and the firm makes a tidy profit ($5600).

their opportunity costs. In actual practice utilities are allowed to earn normal rates of profits roughly equal to the rates of return on similar investments taking into account the need for research, development, and additional investment in new plants and equipment.

MONOPOLISTIC COMPETITION

Monopolies and perfect competitors are, as we have seen, extreme polar opposites. Almost all monopolies are regulated and perfect competitors are found only in a few industries. More common to our everyday experience is **monopolistic competition**, a subtle combination of both. A large number of industries have characteristics of both imperfect competition and monopoly. Firms operating in this market face a downward sloping demand curve and can sell more if they lower price, so the demand for their product is somewhat elastic, more so than a monopolist's. But they also have competitors who will respond in various ways to changes in price. Retail stores such as grocery stores and department stores generally face these conditions, as do most service industries such as cleaners, barber shops, and beauty salons.

 Key Concept: Monopolistic competition is a case in which firms in an industry have some monopolistic power over price but face some competition as well.

Monopolistic competitors control the market up to a certain point. Usually they have a physical location that is convenient to a certain group of customers, or they are able to convince consumers that their product is superior to other similar products, that is, it is differentiated in the consumer's mind, no matter whether there is any real difference between the products. One way to differentiate a product is through advertising. Monopolistic competitors who successfully differentiate can affect their revenues by raising or lowering prices within a certain range. That is, they can usually set their prices above their average unit costs and earn economics profits, at least in the short run. They don't earn as much as a monopolist but more than a perfect competitor.

For example, you probably get your hair cut or styled at a shop near your home where the stylists have probably convinced you that they are the best in town. If they raise their price by, say, 20 percent, you will probably continue to patronize the shop. But if they double their price, you will probably take the trouble to find another barber or stylist even though it means having to travel farther. So the shop has monopoly power over you but only up to a certain point, and also, since they have competitors, they are limited in the amount that they can raise prices. Can you think of other examples? Do you buy a certain brand of bread or soap even though you know it is not really that much different from other brands?

Characteristics of Monopolistic Competition

Monopolistic competition is the term used to describe markets that are competitive but also to some degree monopolistic. The major characteristics of this type of market are:

1. There are large numbers of buyers and sellers in the market. The firms are all relatively small with respect to the total size of the industry.

2. The products in monopolistically competitive industries are differentiated by quality and design differences, advertising, and psychological appeal. Each firm attempts to distinguish its products from those of its competitors. The products are all very close substitutes for one another, but each firm tries to create a monopoly for its product.

3. Firms have limited control over the prices of their products. The firms are small in relation to the market, but they sell a differentiated product. Some consumers are loyal to the unique brands of individual firms, even though there are close substitutes. It is because of this monopoly element that firms have some control over their prices.

4. Entry into the market is relatively easy, although the costs of differentiation can be large for advertising, and so forth. Since the firms are small, relatively small initial investments make entry feasible.

5. Unlike competition, monopolistic competition uses an abundance of advertising. The products are not homogeneous, and advertising exists to convince and persuade consumers about the differences.

Let's now think more carefully about the hairstyling salon discussed above. What makes it different from the perfect competitor it would appear to be? First, it has a partial monopoly over a given location. Customers who want to patronize a competitor will have to spend the time and money, which add up to opportunity costs, to travel further distances. Second, it has a perceived-quality monopoly because for one reason or another we tend to think our barber does a good job, so there is also consumer loyalty involved. Therefore, in a given location barber shops have a partial monopoly over the local market.

Product Differentiation

The hairstylists in our example have a partial monopoly and are protected from competition up to a certain point mostly because they are able to differentiate their product or service in their customers' minds. It is this **product differentiation** more than anything else that distinguishes monopolistic competitors from other forms of market structures.

Key Concept: Product differentiation is the process of psychologically distinguishing among similar products that compete in the same market.

All you have to do to understand them is go to a drugstore. On the shelf you will see four or five different brands of aspirin. Aspirin by itself is a generic product (salicylate) and the same no matter what the brand name. Yet chances are you will find that Bayer ™ aspirin sells for nearly five times as much as lesser-known brands. Why? Because through an expensive and well-thought-out advertising campaign over the years, the Sterling Drug Corporation has managed to convince many people that Bayer aspirin is a superior product. This is not the only one; most retail products are either the same or very similar but differentiated in our minds. Soft drinks, salt, flour, milk, hamburger—all fall into this category.

In fact, almost all wholesale and retail trade, real estate, and personal services—such as legal and medical services—and even a large part of manufacturing including clothing, furniture, and so on fit the monopolistic competition model to the extent that the producers sell very similar products with only slight differences.

Advertising

One key to differentiating products is advertising. American business spends some $120 billion a year on advertising. As a general rule the more similar the product is to its competitors, the more spent on advertising. In the U.S., automobile companies spend the most on advertising, followed closely by soap companies and soft drink producers.

It's easy to get the impression that advertising is a nuisance that we would all be better off without. Much of it, especially the television variety, seems silly and often repetitious. But it's not quite that simple. Advertising does add to business production costs. Spread over a range of output it raises firms' average cost curves and that gets passed on to consumers. Advertising also manipulates us into wanting things we don't really need. But advertising has many positive effects as well.

You will recall from our discussion of consumer demand theory that consumers try to maximize utility by rationally purchasing things that give them the most satisfaction for the price they pay. To do this they must have price and quality information, and advertising can help provide that information. If we didn't have price information, retailers would be able to take advantage of their partial monopoly to charge higher-than-competitive prices. So advertising helps keep prices lower—more competitive—than they would be without it. This is one reason we seldom see lawyers, physicians, dentists, and other professionals advertising their services. They would prefer that price information not be public. If it were, competition would push the price of such services down while, at the same time, these professionals would incur the additional expense of advertising.

From an economic perspective one of the most important effects of advertising is that it tends to create demand. That is, it persuades consumers that they want the product. In our study of consumer demand theory, we noted free market capitalism is guided by consumer sovereignty—the notion that demand begins and ends with the consumer. Producers simply supply what consumers want. But if wants are created by producers—through advertising—rather than coming from the innate desires of consumers, then the validity of the theory of consumer sovereignty comes under question.

The Revised Sequence

This reversal of demand creation is what economist John Kenneth Galbraith has called the "revised sequence." He argues that it is producers who create demand rather than the other way around. Few of us would admit that our desires are conditioned by advertising because, after all, we are smarter than that. Yet, if we think carefully about our perceptions of what quality is, we begin to realize that advertising does, indeed, condition our thinking. Ask yourself, for example, what is the best beer for the money? Then ask yourself: What company spends the most on advertising? Or, what is the best car made in America? Which blue jeans are the best? What is the best personal computer? Or the best breakfast cereal? If you think about it for a minute you will probably agree with Galbraith that our wants are conditioned at least to some degree by our constant exposure to advertising.

Monopolistic competitors, whose products are sold at retail, provide the lion's share of advertising. What they are attempting to do is shift the demand curves for their products rightward where they can sell more at every price. To the extent they are successful, they can increase their revenues and profits.

Efficiency and Monopolistic Competition

Many economists argue that the proliferation of monopolistic competitors tends to promote economic inefficiency. Why position three or four gasoline stations at the same intersection, one on each corner? Or, why does any shopping mall need 29 different shoe stores?

Clearly such examples, which are repeated thousands of times across the country, belie the idealistic notion that competition promotes efficient use of scarce resources. Yet we also have to remember that it is the variety of a wide range of choices that makes life interesting. For that, most of us are willing to pay the costs of advertising and the price of some inefficiency. The extent to which monopolistic competitors are, in fact, inefficient can, however, be logically demonstrated using the tools of economic theory we now have at our disposal.

Monopolistic competitors face the same cost conditions that all firms do. Their average costs decrease at first as they gain efficiencies of scale, but in the long run costs increase as they run into the constraints of size. A retail store is limited in the short run by the size of its showroom, storage space, and even in some cases by the number of cash registers it has. Its cost curves are, therefore, U shaped. But because retailers are partial monopolies, they face downward sloping demand curves; that is, they can only increase sales by lowering prices. They maximize profits if they can set output or sales levels where their marginal costs equal their marginal revenues.

But from the perspective of social welfare, monopolistic competition results in an under-allocation of resources to the production of its goods and services. Since one of the primary characteristics of this market structure is product differentiation, resources also get used up in the advertising and promotion of one product over another. From the perspective of the efficient use of resources by the society, this represents a waste. Compared with the model of competition, then, monopolistic competition falls short of maximizing social welfare.

On the other hand, there are some positive attributes in the functioning of monopolistically competitive markets: relatively free entry by firms when economic profits exist promotes adaptability; resources are reallocated in response to market conditions. Entry also puts downward pressures on prices, as it does in competitive markets. Product differentiation contributes to one of the wonders of the U.S. economy—variety and choice.

OLIGOPOLY

Most major industries in the United States are dominated by only a few large corporations. Judging by the advertising we are subjected to almost everywhere we look, one would think that they are fierce competitors. There isn't much question that Coke and Pepsi are constantly engaged in a battle for their share of a big market; or that Chrysler, General Motors, and Ford spend a lot of money trying to convince us that they build the best cars. Given all that, one has to wonder why their products are priced almost exactly the same. To see why, we need to look at large corporations and how they go about the business of setting their prices and maximizing their profits. Interestingly, these large corporations, although they appear to be competitors, certainly do not conform to the idealized model of perfect competition we examined earlier. Instead, they act more like monopolies than competitors.

The Importance of Oligopolies

By far the most important market structure in the United States and most other advanced industrialized nations is the **oligopoly**: a market with only a few sellers. As a rule of thumb, we consider a market to be an oligopoly if four or fewer firms control at least 50 percent of it. In reality most markets in the U.S. are more concentrated than that. Before foreign automakers entered the market, the auto industry was dominated by only three large corporations; even now most of the aluminum is produced by only two firms; television is dominated by the three major networks; airlines by just six carriers; and so on. These giant corporations that are, indeed, big have some of the characteristics of competitive firms since they do compete through advertising and service. But they more closely resemble monopolies in the sense that they have downward sloping demand curves—that is, if they lower their prices, people will buy more of their product—and they have considerable control over the prices they charge. So, although technically they are not monopolies, what is significant is that they tend to behave as *if* they were and are consistently able to earn economic profits. The reasons for this are analytically somewhat complex and interesting because we all deal with oligopolies every day, and because a large percentage of us either work for one now or will at some time in the future.

 Key Concept: A market is considered an oligopoly if four or fewer firms account for 50 percent or more of sales in that market.

Industry Concentration Ratios

Oligopolistic markets are usually distinguished by a high degree of economic concentration. The degree of concentration in a single market is normally measured by the percentage of total sales (or assets) controlled by the top four firms or, sometimes, the top eight. This is called the four-firm or eight-firm **concentration ratio**. If the four largest firms have more than 50 percent of sales the market is said to be highly concentrated. Many markets in the United States meet this criteria. Among the more interesting examples is the auto rental market, where Hertz, Avis, National, and Budget control 94 percent of auto rentals. In the canned soup market only two firms—Campbell and Heinz—produce 90 percent of all soup consumed. And if you want to buy tennis balls, chances are that you'll buy them from Wilson, Penn, Dunlop, or Spalding because these four firms control 100 percent of the U.S. market.

 Key Concept: A concentration ratio is the percentage of sales or assets controlled by the largest four or eight firms in one market.

One problem here is that concentration ratios do not take into account foreign competition. The U.S. auto industry, for example, is highly concentrated because only three firms account for nearly all of U.S. auto production. But foreign automakers now account for 30 percent of sales in the U.S. market. Another problem arises when regional differences are considered. In some areas one or two firms may dominate the market but not operate at all in other areas. Some of the large regional banks are examples. And in many industries one or two firms may be the only sellers in some cities, making them, in effect, monopolies in that area, but nationally the industry may not be highly concentrated. The newspaper industry is one prominent example. The industry is not concentrated, but in many cities there is only one newspaper, which is effectively a monopoly in that area. But, in general, when the summed concentration ratio exceeds 50 percent, a market can be considered oligopolistically organized.

Characteristics Of Oligopolies

There is great variety in oligopolistic industries, so economists have developed a number of different models of oligopoly to describe their behavior and results. The major characteristics of oligopoly are:

1. The firms in an oligopolistic industry are interdependent. Their pricing and output decisions all affect the other firms in the industry. They all must pay attention to the actions of their rivals. This creates a constant possibility for price wars among oligopolists, or collusion to avoid those price wars. It can also lead to price leadership or a reluctance to alter price. Despite this interdependence, oligopolies do have some control over their prices.

2. A few firms produce most of the output in an industry. These firms are thus usually large with respect to the market, and dominate its activities. Examples include automobiles, computers, steel, aluminum, cigarettes, and chewing gum. In some cases, there may be fewer than ten firms in the entire industry. In others, there may be hundreds of companies, but four or five firms dominate.

3. The product of an oligopoly may be homogeneous or differentiated. If it is a consumer good, it's usually differentiated to gain consumers' attention and loyalty (such as automobiles). And, if it's a raw material sold to other firms, it's usually homogeneous (like steel, copper, or aluminum).

4. There may be technological reasons for domination of an industry by a few firms. Costs may be reduced in large-scale operations. Economies of scale may allow only a few firms to constitute the entire

industry, given the size of the market. Firms may also have grown large due to mergers. As a result, entry into such markets is difficult and a firm must be large to enter.

5. Oligopolies usually have a significant amount of nonprice competition, such as product differentiation and advertising.

The most important thing to understand about oligopolies is that their members are *mutually interdependent*. Any action they take is likely to be matched by their rivals. If one large bank lowers interest rates on loans it knows that all other large banks will be forced to follow. If they don't, they will lose all of their customers. If, for example, a large automaker offers rebates or cash-back incentives, the others almost always follow, and so on. Such interdependence presents the large oligopolistic firm with an entirely different set of problems than those faced by the perfect competitor or the monopolist. To understand why, we look now at pricing strategy in an oligopoly. Then we will be able to draw some conclusions.

The Kinked Demand Curve

There are several theories of how oligopolies behave. The best known is the **kinked demand curve**. Let's assume that an oligopolistic firm with a large share of the industry is producing output Q (as shown in Figure 8-3) and selling its product at a price of P. It also has three rivals, all of whom sell a very similar product at the same price. Now assume that this firm decides to *lower* its price to try to capture a larger market share. What is likely to happen? Most likely its rivals will also lower their prices. Since they all have downward sloping demand curves, lower prices mean increased sales, but each of the four firms will retain their same percentage share of the market. Therefore, assuming that cost conditions remain the same, there is little incentive for oligopolistic firms to lower price, given that they know (or at least are fairly sure) that all their rivals will follow suit. In other words, the oligopolistic firm knows that its demand curve will become inelastic if it attempts to increase profits by cutting price. Therefore, lowering price will reduce total revenues.

 Key Concept: The kinked demand curve shows that since most oligopolies face different elasticities of demand for price changes, their demand curves are kinked at current prices.

On the other hand, if the firm attempts to *raise* price it has no assurance that its rivals will follow. If they hold the line on prices, then the firm may lose a large portion of its present market share to its rivals. So an oligopolistic firm's demand curve is relatively elastic for price increases, but inelastic for price decreases.

The result of all this is to make the oligopolistic firm very uncertain about what will happen if it raises or lowers prices. It only knows that it stands a good chance of losing either way. Therefore, prices in oligopolistic market structures tend to be rigid, seldom fluctuating up and down in response to market conditions as competitive assumptions would suggest they should.

Pricing Strategies

Just because oligopolistic firms do not generally compete with each other on the basis of price does not mean that they do not have pricing strategies. One possible strategy—illegal in the United States—is for all firms in the industry to practice collusion. Executives from all the firms can easily get together for lunch—or a game of golf—and decide on a price increase. If that happens and no one breaks the agreement, then all the firms gain because together they can function exactly as a non-regulated monopoly. Prices could be set at the level where the industry marginal cost curve intersects the industry marginal revenue curve, and profits for all firms would be maximized.

Collusion and Cartels

Outright collusion is illegal in the United States under the antitrust laws, and many executives have gone to jail for attempting it. But around the world it is rather common. The best known example in recent years is the Organization of Petroleum Exporting Countries (OPEC), which meets regularly and publicly to set oil prices and production quotas. The diamond industry is controlled by a **cartel** led by the DeBeers Company in South Africa. And there are many other examples. But, because cartels are illegal in the United States, large oligopolies have developed other, more sophisticated strategies to set prices to attempt to maximize profits.

 Key Concept: A cartel is a group of firms who regularly meet and set prices and marketing strategies.

Price Leadership

One simple and common way to get around the laws against price collusion is for one firm in the industry to take a leadership role in setting prices. When it raises prices the others simply follow. No formal—meaning illegal—agreements are required. There is, instead, a tacit agreement that all firms in the industry will follow the leader. Such price leadership has historically been quite common in the United States. U.S. Steel used to set steel prices and all

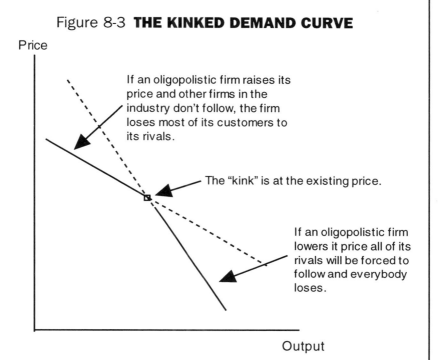

Figure 8-3 **THE KINKED DEMAND CURVE**

Price

If an oligopolistic firm raises its price and other firms in the industry don't follow, the firm loses most of its customers to its rivals.

The "kink" is at the existing price.

If an oligopolistic firm lowers it price all of its rivals will be forced to follow and everybody loses.

Output

Firms in oligopolistic markets face different elasticity responses for price increases than for price decreases. If the firm increases its selling price its rivals will tend not to follow, so its demand curve for price increases is relatively elastic. If the firm lowers its selling price its rivals will tend to follow, so its demand curve for a price decrease is relatively inelastic. Therefore, there is a tendency for prices to be rigid in oligopolistic markets.

other steel companies would change prices equivalent to U.S. Steel's price. **Price leadership** was also common in the tobacco and food industries for many years. Recently, however, foreign competition has broken up such tacit agreements and most oligopolies are forced to match their foreign competitors (many of whom are part of cartels in their own countries) if they want to stay in business.

Key Concept: Price leadership occurs when one firm increases prices and all others in the industry follow.

Decreasing Average Costs

While the kinked demand curve hypothesis and game theory pricing strategies do help us understand price rigidity under oligopoly, they are not a total explanation of oligopolistic behavior. In fact, a comprehensive explanation of how and why oligopolies behave the way they do is a challenge still facing economists. A brief look at the behavior of average cost curves and their relation to efficiency and economies of scale will help us further understand how oligopolistic firms maintain their market shares.

As we saw in Chapter 7, large firms tend to have declining average costs over a wide range of output. This is because their larger size allows them to take advantage of the efficiencies that come with economies of scale, especially over the long run. This is true only up to a certain point, however, since size eventually becomes difficult to manage efficiently or resources become scarce.

It would seem logical, therefore, that in an oligopolistic market situation the firm with the lowest average costs would continue increasing output until it puts its rivals out of business. But look at Figure 8-4. If the firm is producing at output level E (where it maximizes profits because its marginal revenue equals its marginal cost, point H), then its profits are the rectangle ABCD.[2] But if it increases production beyond level E, its total profits decline until it reaches output level F, where MC = AC = P = AR. At this point it no longer earns economic profits because its price is equal to its average cost per unit. This would put the oligopoly in the position of a regulated monopoly or a perfect competitor, earning only normal profits equal to its opportunity costs.

Therefore, the larger firms in an oligopolistic industry have little incentive to initiate price competition. Indeed, from their point of view, it would be irrational. Oligopolies, therefore, are generally content to operate at less than capacity with a given share of the market, knowing that they are maximizing their profits. The low level of their cost curves assures that no one else can enter the industry. This is one reason why it is so difficult for new industries in the smaller, less-developed countries to compete with firms in the highly industrialized areas, and why large oligopolies have gained so much power in the world economy.

Barriers to Entry

Declining average costs over a wide range of production present smaller firms who would like to enter an oligopolistic market with considerable

---

[2]   This is because its total revenues are price times quantity, or the rectangle OBCE. Its total costs are average cost times quantity, or the rectangle OADE. Therefore, total profits are total revenue minus total cost, or OBCE–OADE.

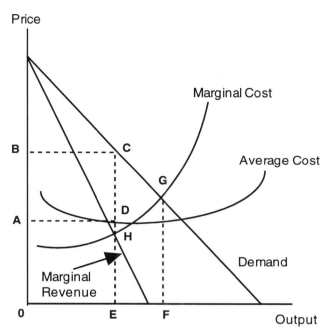

Figure 8-4
RESTRICTED OUTPUT OLIGOPOLISTIC PRICING

If oligopolies were price competitive they would increase production to output level F, where MC = P = AR. This would result in a perfectly competitive outcome. However, because they face downward sloping demand and marginal revenue curves they maximize their profits by producing where MR = MC, at the lower level of output E and a higher price OB, where profits are the rectangle ABCD. From a social welfare point of view the result is a lower level of output sold at a higher price.

barriers to entry. No small firm can produce at cost levels even approaching the low costs large firms can achieve from mass production techniques. Thus, once a firm gains a foothold in an industry and/or the market is shared by 3 or 4 large firms, others are effectively prohibited from entering. But with the increase of foreign competition in recent years that has all changed dramatically. The gradual erosion of the U.S. auto industry is perhaps the most familiar example.

Key Concept: Barriers to entry exist when a few large firms dominate an industry and enjoy the efficiencies of mass production and economies of scale.

THE CASE FOR OLIGOPOLY

It is easy to think that because oligopolies are difficult for new firms to enter and because they restrict output and thus tend to earn more than normal profits—given they restrict output, enjoy low costs, and economies of scale— they are less than perfect members of our economic society. And, they are roundly criticized from many quarters. But we could also argue that oligopolies perform an important and useful function in a capitalist society.

Efficiency

Many large scale oligopolies evolved because they were more efficient than their competitors. Low average costs over the long run may mean high profit levels, but they also mean that prices in general are lower than they would be under conditions where a large number of small firms are trying to produce the same product with much higher average costs.

Also, some economists, such as the aforementioned Mr. Galbraith, argue that large oligopolies are able to devote much larger amounts of investment to research and development and are, therefore, the driving force in technological change and innovation.

Oligopolies and Politics

Oligopolies are one of the most controversial issues in all of economics, to say nothing of the political interest they stimulate. Many economists and others argue that the large oligopolies should be broken up into smaller, more competitive units. Doing this, they say, would result in more efficient production and lower prices. Others, however, argue that the large corporations have such an advantage in terms of technical efficiency that it is unrealistic to think about breaking them up. Instead, they suggest that increased government control would assure more responsible behavior. Still other economists argue that the large oligopolies should be taken over and run by the government, thus taking advantage of economies of scale without the disadvantage of excess profits accruing to a privileged group. This controversy is far from settled.

SUMMARY

✓ Monopoly is an often misunderstood concept. Most monopolies are natural monopolies in the sense that there isn't any other rational way to organize production. Utilities, such as electricity, gas, and telephone companies are the most common examples.

✓ Since monopolies are the only sellers in a given market, they face downward sloping demand curves, which means they must lower price to increase sales.

✓ If left to their own desires, monopolies would set their production levels where MC = MR, the profit maximization point for any firm. This point, for monopolies, gives the highest price the market will bear. But because this would give them very high profits they are usually regulated by governmental agencies and forced to produce at a level where their average costs equal price. They are then permitted normal profits.

✓ Many monopolies, however, practice some form of price discrimination in the sense that they charge different prices to different groups of customers, thus transferring some of the consumer surplus to themselves.

✓ Monopolistic competitors have some of the characteristics of monopolies and some of perfect competitors. They have some monopolistic control over their markets through location of product differentiation. Differentiation comes about through location, image, quality differences and so on. It may be enhanced by advertising.

✓ Advertising raises production costs, which are passed on to consumers. But it also performs the function of disseminating price and quality information, which fosters competition.

✓ Advertising is perceived by some to reverse the normal sequence of demand creation. That is, our desires are shaped by producers rather than by our basic wants and needs. This process is called "the reversed sequence."

✓ Monopolistic competition tends to be inefficient in the sense that it promotes excess capacity. However, it also enlarges the range of variety and consumer choice.

✓ Oligopolistic markets are those dominated by a few large firms. The basic characteristics of an oligopolistic market structure are: a) a few firms produce most of the output in an industry; b) they are large enough to have extensive economies of scale; and c) the firms are interdependent in terms of their pricing and output decisions.

✓ The mutual interdependence of oligopolistic firms means that there is little incentive for them to lower price because they know that others will follow. On the other hand, oligopolistic firms cannot raise prices for fear that their rivals won't follow. Therefore, some oligopolies face a kinked demand curve.

✓ In the absence of regulation and antitrust laws the pricing strategy of an oligopolist might well involve collusion, an agreement with the competition to fix or set prices, or perhaps even the formation of a cartel, a group of producers who formally agree upon output levels and prices to control a market. Such activities are currently illegal in the United States. Thus a practice used by some oligopolistic firms in the United States is price leadership, where one firm takes the lead in establishing prices and the others follow.

✓ Mergers and acquisitions, as we saw in the beer and tire industries, allow for some entry and, importantly, increased concentration in oligopolistic industries. In addition, global competition and capital mobility have significantly changed the dynamics of entry into oligopolistic industries.

✓ The case for oligopoly is made largely on the grounds of the efficiency that comes with large size and economies of scale even though profit rates tend to be higher than normal.

NEW VOCABULARY

price maker	the kinked demand curve
natural monopolies	cartel
monopolistic competition	price leadership
product differentiation	barriers to entry
oligopoly	

QUESTIONS FOR REVIEW

1. What is the difference between a pure monopoly and a pure competitor?
2. How is a monopoly a "price maker?"
3. Do monopolies maximize profits?
4. Why are monopolies usually regulated or owned by the government?
5. What are some examples of monopolistic competitors?
6. What are some examples of product differentiation?
7. What are the basic characteristics of an oligopolistic market structure?
8. Describe why oligopolistic firms are mutually interdependent.
9. What is the rationale of a pricing strategy for oligopolistic firms?
10. Explain how price leadership works in oligopolistic market structures.

Glossary

Assets: what a business owns.

Average total costs: the sum of average variable costs and average fixed costs at any level of output.

Average variable costs: total variable costs divided by units of output.

Balance sheet: shows what a company owns compared to what it owes.

Depreciation: an estimate of the portion of a long-term asset's value that is used up in one particular period.

Barriers to entry: a few large firms dominate an industry and enjoy the efficiencies of mass production and economies of scale.

Capitalism: an economic system based on private ownership of the factors of production and on free markets that determine what should be produced.

Cartel: a group of firms who regularly meet and set prices and marketing strategies.

Ceteris paribus: in experimental situations only one variable at a time can be changed while all others are held constant.

Complementary goods: those in which a change in price of one will cause the demand for both to move in the opposite direction. That is, there is an inverse relationship between price and quantity demanded.

Concentration ratio: the percentage of sales or assets controlled by the largest four or eight firms in one market.

Consumer needs: food, shelter, and clothing. Wants are determined by cultural conditioning.

Consumer sovereignty: the idea that decisions about what to produce are dictated by consumers' desires.

Consumer surplus: the bonus you get from paying the market price instead of a price equal to your own money-utility equation.

Corporations: businesses that have the same legal responsibility as individuals but are owned by a group of stockholders who appoint managers to be responsible for the operation of the business.

Depreciation: refers to the practice of estimating the portion of an asset's value that is used up each year and then showing it as an expense so you can see how much of an asset's worth was sacrificed in a particular year to earn revenue.

Distribution: the process of allocating goods and services to various groups and individuals.

Dividends: distributions of earnings to the stockholders of a business.

Entrepreneurship: the ability to combine land, labor, and capital with technological know-how to produce goods and services with the objective of profit and the risk of loss.

Equilibrium: the point where there are no shortages or surpluses and the market clears at the equilibrium price.

Expenses: the dollar value of those resources sacrificed to generate revenues.

Expenses: the cost of materials and services used up in the course of getting revenue. Also called the "cost of doing business."

Factor market: a market in which firms demand natural resources, labor, capital, and know-how from the individuals and households who own them. Factor resources are used to produce goods and services.

Factors of production: land, labor, physical and financial capital, and the entrepreneurial skills to get them organized to produce goods and services.

Fallacy of composition: the logical error of assuming that what may work for one will work for all.

Financial leverage: how much a company is borrowing in relation to its equity.

Financial statements: provide specific information about a business's status on a particular date and its activities during a specific period.

Fixed costs: a firm's costs that must be paid even if the firm is not producing.

Income statement: compares total income to total expenses. The difference between the two is net earnings, or net profit—the so-called "bottom line."

International economics: the study of the trading of goods and services between nations and of the international financial system that facilitates this trade.

Journal entry: uses debits and credits to show the changes in asset, liability, or equity accounts as the result of an economic event.

Kinked demand curve: since most oligopolies face different elasticities of demand for price changes, their demand curves are kinked at current prices.

Law of Demand: the general observation that as prices are lowered for a given product, consumers will want to purchase more of it.

Law of Diminishing Returns: when the amount of one input is fixed while others are varied, the marginal product of all inputs will at some point begin to decline.

Law of Supply: as the price of any given product is increased, producers will want to supply more of it.

Ledgers: group together all the changes in a particular account in one place.

Liabilities: what a business owes.

Equity: the value of the owner's stake in a business.

Long-run average cost curves: the combination of short-run average cost curves as measured over a longer time period.

Long-run equilibrium: under perfect competition marginal revenue (price), marginal costs, and average costs are all equal.

Macroeconomics: the study of the overall levels of employment, national output and income, and how they can be controlled.

Marginal cost: the extra cost involved in producing one additional unit.

Marginal revenue: the additional revenue received from the sale of one unit of product.

Marginal utility: the amount of satisfaction gained by consuming one additional unit of a product.

Microeconomics: the study of the allocation of scarce resources among competing ends. It deals primarily with the operation of business firms and the behavior of consumers in a market setting.

Monopolistic competition: a case in which firms in an industry have some monopolistic power over price but face some competition as well.

Natural monopolies: generally utilities such as electricity, gas, water, and telephone companies.

Oligopoly: four or fewer firms account for 50 percent or more of sales in a market.

Opportunity cost: the cost of the next best foregone alternative.

Partnerships: businesses owned by two or more persons who share responsibility for it.

Perfect competition: all economic transactions are conducted in an auction setting. Neither sellers nor buyers can influence prices.

Price leadership: one firm increases prices and all others in the industry follow.

Price-earnings ratio: a company's current stock price divided by its current estimated earnings per share.

Price maker: a firm that has sufficient control over its market to set its selling price and level of output to its advantage.

Price takers: firms in a perfectly competitive industry that are so small they have no influence over the market price.

Principle of diminishing marginal utility: the idea that consuming additional units of anything in a given time period will give you less additional satisfaction.

Private property: a system in which individuals have the right to keep, use, or sell the goods they produce or legally acquire.

Product differentiation: the process of psychologically distinguishing similar products that compete in the same market.

Product market: a market in which a particular good or service is bought and sold.

Production function: the rate of increase in output as a result of varying the level of inputs used.

Retained earnings: that portion of profits retained for reinvestment in the corporation for expansion.

Return on sales: net income divided by sales.

Revenues: the dollar value of the resources flowing in as the result of an exchange.Capital: Two meanings—real capital is plant and equipment; financial capital is the money needed to control the factors of production.

Scientific method: a procedure that uses experimentation to test hypotheses against reality.

Securities and Exchange Commission: the governmental agency charged with overseeing and regulating the financial markets.

Sole proprietorships: businesses owned by one individual who bears total responsibility for its operation.

Specialization: the process of allocating specific tasks to different people to accomplish a given goal.

Substitutable goods: those in which a change in the price of one will cause the demand for the other to move in the same direction. That is, there is a direct relationship between price and quantity.

Total profit: total revenue minus total cost.

Total revenue: the summation of marginal revenue, or price times quantity sold.

Total utility: the sum of the satisfaction gained by consuming a given number of units of a product.

Utility: the amount of satisfaction one gets from consuming or having a product.

Venture capitalists: investors who focus on investing in new, often risky, business ventures.

Index